For someone like me who doe

could do this, it's made it really easy for me, step by step and actually get it done. So super happy and thanks for everything!

– Alana Carpenter, Author of *Why Men Made me Fat*

I've done everything I needed to do, I've actually completed all the work on the weekend all ready for transcription and what helped was the pre-work we had to do. I'm just really, really excited now to get my book in my hands.

– Anthony Kilner, Author of *Secret Spiritual Business*

This weekend has been amazing. I never had the courage or how-to but through doing this course with Nat, it's given me everything I needed to make my book a reality.

– Debbie Severiny, Author of *I'm in Business – Now What?*

I've just completed my Ultimate 48-Hour Author Weekend and it's been a remarkable experience. It's just something I didn't even think possible until this opportunity came up that Natasa's created and put together a weekend, it's really one of those things which is an opportunity that can't be missed.

– Despina Karatzias, Author of *Adventures of a Balloon Girl*

I've just completed the 48-Hour Author Weekend, and what can I say? It's been absolutely mind blowing and what a wonderful experience. The venue was just amazing; every little corner I discovered had the wow factor and really the highlight for me was just how educational the weekend was.

– Dora Altintas, Author of *The 7 Deadly Sins of Customer Service*

I've got to say, what a fantastic weekend! I've completed my book within 48 Hours and it's been an extraordinary experience. Right from the beginning all the way through has been absolutely sensational. I just want to say a heartfelt thank you.

– John Sharkey, Author of *Quest to Freedom*

This weekend has been phenomenal; I'm actually going to be publishing my book at the start of next year and I'm so excited. What have I got to say about this weekend? It's been relaxed, educational and inspiring. Oh yeah, and the house and the food's been totally awesome.

– Nicole Stacewicz, Author of *Insider Tips on Internet Marketing*

It's been wonderful, the structure has been amazing, the pre-work really set us up for success the whole time and the community spirit, everybody supporting each other. It's been a fantastic experience, thoroughly recommend it, if you've got a book in you, you've got to do this. I got it done! It's all uploading to Dropbox right now.

– Russell Scott, Author of *Free Time*

I can highly recommend this weekend for anyone to do it because at the end of the day, I came in with my intention and I fulfilled it. I've even got a second book now ready to rock and roll and once you learn the system you can just go and do it. So I would just say, just do it! Go for it!

– Sabrina Muller, Author of *Confessions of a Weight Loss Junkie*

I've just completed the 48-hour Ultimate Author weekend and it's been an enormous experience, it's going to really kick start my book, I'm right up to the end, I've just got a couple more hours to complete it and it's going to be out there and on its way. I am just so excited.

– Sonia Scomazzon, Author of *What Parent Repress Children Express*

Ultimate 48 Hour Author

Natasa Denman

First published by Busybird Publishing 2014

ISBN 978-0-9923576-8-9

Bound and printed by

National Library of Australia Cataloguing-in-Publication entry

Author: Denman, Natasa, author.

Title: Ultimate 48 hour author / Natasa Denman.

ISBN: 9780992357689 (paperback)

Subjects: Business writing.

Authorship.

Dewey Number: 808.06665

Edited and Published by Busybird Publishing

Cover image by Kev Howlett

Cover design by Busybird Publishing

Layout and typesetting: Jason Farrugia

Typeset in Helvetica Neue 11.5/16

Busybird Publishing
PO Box 855
Eltham Victoria
Australia 3095

Dedication

To my Outstanding Family for their tremendous support in writing this book and building our Businesses. My children Judd and Mika who are a driving force behind my motivation, my husband Stuart for being the best dad and right hand man and my mum who steps up in the times we need to be out serving other business owners to create amazing businesses through publishing their books.

Contents

Introduction

The story of the Ultimate 48-hour author started in late 2012 when the partner of one of my businesses, the Ninja Business Chicks and I decided to go away in early 2013 and write our book, *Ninja Couch Marketing*.

We set out a plan that we were going to do this in one weekend. I even sat down and mapped out when we would do our writing sessions and when we would have our breaks, until a few days before that weekend I discovered a way that would really fast track this process.

That way will be revealed to you later in the book. More importantly in this introduction I really want to cover off with you why is it so important to have a book if you are a business owner, specifically if you want to be a successful entrepreneur. I will tell you about my experiences, because I think that's very important: I'm a very big believer that the being comes with the doing, so anything that I do within my businesses is something that I have done myself, and I would never think of asking anyone to do anything that I wouldn't do myself.

So when I originally started out in business in May of 2010, having been an employee for the previous 13 years, I started out as a weight loss coach. My very first business (and still a business that I operate in nowadays) is called "Ultimate Weight Loss, Lose the Last 10 Kilos."

For the first 12 months I really worked hard to get this business off the ground. I only had 2-3 clients and a measly $7000 by the time year one finished. So what did I do? About six months in someone came in and said, "You know what, Nat? You have a lot of awesome information that you could share with people. Why don't you write a book?" Well, from that moment … I always say never plant an idea in my head, because I'll be sure to action it if I think for a second it's a great idea.

So I did, I set a goal in January of 2011 and in 90 days I completed my first book and it was out within the first six months of that year. This is what was the turning point within my business Ultimate Weight Loss and as soon as the book came out, funnily enough, my daughter was born pretty much as soon as I received that book. I was having my second child and what happened was the flood gates opened; people started wanting a piece of me and really wanting to work with me as a coach, specifically in that area of weight loss. So I had no choice, because I really wanted to completely let go of my day job; and I started coaching people a mere three weeks after having my second baby.

I did everything between breastfeeds. I'd go and coach a client and I'd go back upstairs since my office is underneath my house. I'd go to a networking event, come back, breast feed the baby and so on it went for months because with both of my children I'd always set a goal that I'd breast feed them until they were 12 months old. So, a huge commitment on both parts, being a brand new mum of a second child, having a three-year old as well as working everything around my husband's schedule as he was still working full time.

Chapter 1

The Master Plan

Having a master plan for your book goal and bringing your book into reality is the very first step that we need to address in order for you to be successful in bringing your book into reality in just 48 Hours. There are two components in this chapter that I really want to discuss in a lot of detail with you.

I want to teach you how to set goals properly and what I'm going to teach you is how to set your goal in terms of when your book will be finished. With your draft and having your goal for when your book will be in your hands as a reality. Then I want you to come up with a timeline and a plan what you are going to action in terms of bringing those goals to fruition as well as doing it effectively, easily and really effortlessly by knowing what these steps are.

The journey to success is not about luck; it truly is a logical sequence of steps that you need to take. Some people get there sooner and some people get there faster. It all depends upon our abilities, resources, talents and many other variables that create a journey that is different for every single person. What works for one person may not work for another, however there are certain things that have been around for centuries now that are common amongst successful people and one of those is goal setting.

So why do so many people not set goals? In fact the percentages are that 95-97% of people don't set goals that leaves a mere 3-5% of people that do. If you have a look at our world population and the abundance around us you generally see that percentage as reality in terms of how much poverty there is in our world being say around that 95-97% and then the abundance and the riches residing in only 3-5% of the population.

There was a study on Yale University graduates that was conducted when they were leaving the university and they followed them through a 20-year period. There was a group of 100 students and after 20 years they revisited them and found out that the 3-5% of the students that had goal set had a higher net worth than the other 95-97%. Now that is pretty astonishing!

I really want you to focus on becoming a master goal setter, which is what I'm going to teach you in this chapter. This is what I'm very passionate about and what has worked for me for the last 15 years. As far back as I can remember, I have been setting goals. Not in the system that I will teach you now which is a lot more effective and specific.

Every New Year I would get my gifts from my parents; I'd get a new diary. In that new diary I would write down about 10-15 different things that I wanted to achieve for the following year. Now I never referred back to it, however towards the end of that year I would have a look at that and I would see that I did achieve 80% of what was there. That's what my aim is for you as well. There's no perfection; I don't believe in perfection.

Even though when you look at other people's books they may seem like they're perfect. What I want to tell you is this – aim to be 80%. Aim for the 80-20 rule because perfection is all about looping and insanity. So let things go!

Aim to provide quality content and for it to be organised well, however, let go of that perfectionism bone that you may have in your body and you will see yourself and your success in your life propel you a lot further forward without worrying about every single intricate detail.

By setting goals you are truly starting with the end in mind. When I originally wrote my first book, I will share with you the goal that I set later on so you will understand the template that I want to teach you how you should set them for yourself. By setting a goal and creating a plan you truly end up making a commitment to yourself. The strongest commitment that we can make is the one that we make to ourselves; always, always remember that. Because you're not cheating anyone else but yourself if you don't follow through!

One of my favourite sayings is if you plan to fail you fail to plan. As simple as this sounds it's 100% accurate.

You're really creating this master plan that I'm going to teach you in this chapter. It will make managing this project a lot easier. A lot of people don't write a book because of the enormous, gigantic mountain of a task that is ahead of them. They see that as complicated and not something that they can manage themselves. My whole purpose behind writing this book is actually to give you the really easy steps to follow so again, we're revisiting that success is not about luck. It's actually a system that makes it easy.

It is a system and there are logical steps to follow in order to bring about what you want in reality, including in this instance your book.

What your plan and your goals will allow you to do is create that timeline. So there you go; the first step is to set that goal, then have the plan, and then you go onto the timeline. This is the action list of things that you need to execute in order to make your book a reality. That is the only way your book will come into reality rather than stay stuck inside your head.

Remember, the power of putting pen to paper is not to be underestimated, because it's that connection between your mind and your physical body. What happens is that you end up embedding what you want in your subconscious mind, which in turn will go to action to make your goal come true. In this case bringing your book into reality.

I really want you to associate yourself with the exercise of setting goals. Here I just want to address why people do set goals and why so many people don't. It is because it's become so familiar, the concept of goal setting that people tend to just ignore it. Oh, here we go, goal setting again! They underestimate the power of it. I'm here to tell you that it works, it has worked for me for decades now and it continues to just propel me to higher and higher levels of success.

Setting goals work in every area of my life. I'm not just talking about financial success. I'm talking about health, about relationships even being a parent. I'm talking about other interests in personal development that I have and focus on in my life. We're not just talking about abundance and success in our business lives. Of course that is what we're focusing on here; that is what you'd love to get as a result of writing a book and I will teach you exactly how to do that but always remember that goal setting is a lot more than just about setting goals within your business.

So let's get into it. What I'm going to give you help with now is to set your goals effectively and how to also calibrate yourself. What often happens is people will set goals and they may not achieve them. I ask this question and I often have a lot of clients that I mentor myself. I'll have a look at their initial 90-day goals and I see how unrealistic they are, because they're just starting out and they really don't know how they should set them. A few weeks later, a couple of months later we have a look at them, and often at times they're a little bit far-fetched so we bring them back a little bit.

And that's exactly what happened to me. I remembered in my first year of starting my business I wanted to generate $100,000! Little did I know exactly how much work and effort and foundation building needs to happen to get to that six figure income. It took me about 2 1/2 years to get to that point, however I never gave up. I pulled it right back and what I did is then made my goals be more realistic.

This brings me to the system.

Now most of you will have heard of the SMART template and if you haven't heard of the SMART template it stands for setting Specific – Measurable – Attractive - Realistic and Time-Bound goals. Therefore all of those attributes need to be addressed within your goal.

Using this template, I included a couple of additional prerequisites. Those were that your goals must be written in the present tense as if you're already in possession of them as well as including your modalities so addressing your visual, kinaesthetic and auditory modalities. Make it in terms of what will you feel, hear and see when you have achieved your goal.

What I would like to do now is share with you my goal around writing my very first book and how that looked like and then I want to give you the template to do it for yourself. I'm happy for you to photocopy out of this book to do it many, many times over for all the areas of your life. The key point is that you model what I did, because often times my clients do model the areas that I set my goals around because they say, "I want to be just like you so I'm just going to set goals exactly how you do it and I can get exactly the same results as you". That is one of the success principles around modelling excellence; so if someone's got the results you want to achieve do what they do and you most likely will achieve that same result with a little practice.

I set goals in five key areas. Business/career, health/wellness, career/

personal development, family/relationships and financial/materialistic goals.

For the purpose of your book, I would love for you to set your goal for when you finish the draft of your book that is when you have recorded and finished it over a 48-hour weekend. Think about what date it is? Say that you've completed all your files and all the bits and pieces that I will ask you to do in the following chapters. Then in the second goal I want you to also set the goal of when you're actually holding your published book in your hands.

So here is my goal for when I was writing my very first book. *The 7 Ultimate Secrets to Weight Loss*.

"It is the 31st of March 2011 and I have just completed 90 pages in Word on my very first book, *The 7 Ultimate Secrets to Weight Loss*. I feel proud of myself. I see the first draft in my hands and I hear myself saying, "Oh my God! I have just written a book!" "

Your Book Goal

Name: ______________________________

Weekend Book Goal:

It is the ____________ and I have ______________________________
____
____
____

I feel ______________________________

I hear ______________________________

I see ______________________________

Published Book Goal:

It is the ____________ and I have ______________________________
____
____
____

I feel ______________________________

I hear ______________________________

I see ______________________________

So as you can see, I wrote the goal in the present tense. It was specific and measurable and it was quite realistic. When I was setting the goal I said to myself, I want to achieve 90 pages in 90 days and I did this in the traditional way. I actually sat down and typed it on my computer and spent all those hours that I no longer spend wasting time. This is why I'm teaching you so you don't have to do what I did the very first time.

That's the beauty of it. When someone has discovered a faster, more simple and effortless way of doing something, especially the system behind writing a book in 48 hours, once you understand the concepts that I will teach in the upcoming chapters you will want to model that. Now I have perfected the system, I could write a book in a day. As long as I have the chapters unpacked and I have got the outline and everything that I've spent the time planning, I can literally punch out a book in one day.

That is how I want you to set your goals. Make sure that again they're realistic; they're specific and definitely set that time. Use that template and go for it and now set both of your book writing goals.

When you have set those goals the next step is to chunk everything down. So what does that mean? That means that you want to break it right down into smaller weekly goals. Your actions that you will take to bring into reality your book before the weekend, there will be some pre-work that you will need to complete. In the upcoming chapters you will find out what that pre-work is and why it is required.

It generally takes between 6-10 hours for you to get yourself ready for your Ultimate 48 Hour Author Weekend. What I would love for you to do is chunk it right down to 1 hour preparation sessions.

Let's say you were going away in six weeks' time, what I would love for you to do is find two one-hour slots in your diary that you will schedule with yourself to spend on writing or unpacking your book as well as doing some logistics around preparation for the weekend. There's going to be a checklist that I will give you that you will need to follow for the pre-work that happens before the 48 Hour Weekend.

So chunk it down and I think Tony Robbins said this, "What gets scheduled gets done!" and without knowing that he originally said that, I often have said to my family, please whatever you do if you're going to ask me to do it for you, get me to open up my diary and put it in there. If it's in there it's going to get done. If you just tell me and I don't actually note it down, it will likely slip my mind and I won't do it. Not because I don't want to, but because I have a million things going on all at once.

It is the same thing with your preparation hours. If you don't schedule them, you're more likely to slack off and actually not follow through. So schedule those two one-hour sessions. If your weekend is six weeks away, sit down and put a timer on. When you actually put a timer on that one hour that you have, you will see your productivity and effectiveness quadruple. The pressure that you will be under to punch out a certain amount of words or planning makes you work faster and more effectively. Trust me on that one!

What you want to be doing in that one-hour session is spending half the time on your unpacking of the chapters and then half the time on some logistics work. If you want to have illustrations in your book or you need to order some graphic design or you need to gain some testimonials from all the clients, whatever it is that is on the pre book weekend checklist that is one of the things that you need to be completing during these preparation sessions.

My favourite saying is *consistency is king*. Be consistent over this period leading up to the book weekend. Even if you do small increments over a long period of time, they build up into this massive project that you will achieve for yourself that will change not just your business, but also, ultimately, your life.

That is what a book does and as much as people think they're just doing it for their business, I believe that the benefits personally as an individual is in increasing your own self-worth. It's a sense of pride and achievement that not many people can say they have done. You may hear people around the place saying, "Oh, you know I'm writing a book!" maybe in that community, but believe me and trust me when I say this, many people talk about it but not many people do it.

So be one of those less than 3% of people that are actually going to follow through and bring their own book into reality.

One other tip that I want to give you is how you can become more productive and effective is to start doing a 'top six list' each day for your life and your business. Get yourself a little notepad that you can use and write down the numbers 1 through to 6. Each night before you finish up for the day, write yourself the 'top six list' for the next day and focus on things that are highest priority to lowest priority.

If you don't finish your top six things then move them across to the next day and aim to finish them then. Why six? Because six is not too many but not to few! It's not going to overwhelm you and it's not too little so that you end up being stretched to a point where you actually really punching out considerable amount of work and propelling yourself forward to that success and definitely bringing your book into reality.

It works, it has worked for many successful people; this is where I picked that up from. I actually read this tip within a Mary K Ash book, *Miracles Happen* and she called it the $35,000 list. There is quite a story behind it so if you want to refer to that look up her book. I thought it was really, really amazing and I followed it and have done it for myself ever since. Again, don't be afraid to model what works for others. It is the quickest way to get their results!

Finally what I want to address before I give you your homework as part of this chapter, is some of the objections that people come up with around setting goals and creating plans. One of the biggest ones is, "What if I don't follow through on my plan and achieve my goals?" Often I look a little bit deeper at this and I've done a lot of reading of teachings by Doctor John D Martini and he talks a lot about values and his core message is how important our values are in our life. We spend most of our time within what are our highest values. In my life my highest value is my business and education and that is where I spend the majority of my time and I have this as he calls it 'attention surplus disorder'.

Other things like cooking or housecleaning that are really, really low down on my values list are where I have that 'attention deficit disorder'. So what I want to say about this is if you don't follow through on your plan in terms of your book, I would say return to your compelling reason why and then come up with 100 reasons how having a published book will assist you in your business in your life. You need to really build up the value behind having this book in your life and for your business and therefore what that will do if book writing was number nine in your list of values by giving yourself 100 reasons how it will assist your higher values.

Let's say your business was my business, I would say "Well a book will position me as an expert. A book will give me credibility. A book will increase my self-worth" and I would keep going and going until I came up with 100 reasons. A book will assist me financially so that I would have a better life and be able to help my children get awesome education. Things like that are examples of what you want to write for yourself. Other things to look at if you're not following through on your goals and your intentions is to review, are you already happy where you are, at the moment? If you're already happy, why would you do anything different?

Think about that for a minute and then follow that through with a question, *well are you really?* I really want you to reflect on yourself and I want you to look at where you are. As far as I have studied and know about human behaviour is that we're driven by goals. Even if we don't set them we still have goals and visions for our lives.

When we set them, we're more in control. That's the beauty of planning and having goals. Three and a half years ago before I started all my businesses, back then it was one and now there's four, things seem to happen by chance. Now they happen by choice! When you goal set and create plans, you are actually in charge of your destiny. Nothing else is controlling you and there are not many surprises. At least if there are surprises, you're in control and you're in power so that is the difference.

Change is not by chance, change is by choice when you actually create goals and set out plans.

Ensure that you follow the templates and if you do the actions that are set out throughout this book, I have no doubt that you will be successful at bringing your book into reality. The last thing I wanted to mention is to move yourself away from distractions.

Did you know that it actually takes 20 minutes to come back and regroup from a moment when you are distracted then coming back to the original task that you were doing? My tip around this is to plan some alone time. Alone time is very, very important. This is probably where we do the bulk of our effective work.

So set out in your days some hours where you can be fully alone and undistracted. Put your phone on do not disturb or airplane mode, because even vibrations can be very distracting and the little blips that come up often on computers nowadays. Other times where you can fit in some alone time late at night – for those of you that are night owls – and very early in the morning, so two hours before everyone else gets up. Usually in that 5am-7am time slot if you are a morning person.

And remember, interruptions are the enemy of productivity!

Ultimate actions for this chapter:

1. Write your book goals using the SMART method, writing your goals in the present tense as if you're in possession of them and using the visual-kinaesthetic-auditory modalities to explain what you will feel, hear and see.
2. Create your timeline and actions you will take weekly to be successful at bringing your book into reality.
3. Break it all down, write in those weekly and two one-hour blocks that you will do each week in planning and the work that you will do towards your book unpack.

Chapter 2

Prep for 48-Hour Success

Now that you've done your master plan around your goal-setting as well as the breakdown there are certain things that you must complete in order to be successful when you go away for your 48 Hour Weekend to write and complete your book.

Why the preparation?

Well, in order for you to be able to do it in 48-hours, you will need to have certain things that you have completed as we've mentioned in chapter 1. You will need to have done the 6-10 hours of pre-work to get all your ideas, research and logistics around a book completed. This is what will give you the complete system for you to be successful at the weekend. You will save time because you will get those logistics out of the way and organised so that you can then focus on your marketing post the writing weekend.

You will be able to find and utilise the tools, people and resources that you need to have in order for your 48-hours to run smoothly and the beauty of this is I want to give you a checklist that you will follow. You can hold yourself accountable and watch yourself progress to success prior to the weekend. By completing your pre 48 Hour Author checklists you will have the confidence and certainty and as you come to the end of this checklist this will increase. You will have knowledge within yourself that you will be successful at the weekend.

So take it one step at a time, we're now onto chapter 2 and within this chapter we really want to take you through this particular checklist. You can be prepared and understand what each item on this checklist means. So let's get started.

Pre 48 Hour Author Weekend Checklist	
	Done ✓
Be Clear on Your Purpose for the Book	
Be Clear on The Target Market & The Problem	
Book Title Chosen or 4-5 Options for Feedback	
All Chapters and Sexy Names for them Outlined	
All Chapters Unpacked	
Facts and Statistics	
Stories/Metaphors	
Why (Min 5 Benefits for Each topic), What, How, What If	
Plan for your Introduction and Afterward	
Thoughts around the Design of Book Cover	
Collect 10 Testimonials from past Clients	
Think about a Dedication for Your Book	
Come up with your Programs/Offers that will go at the back	
Write Your Bio	
Write the Synopsis for the Back of the Book	
Choose any 'Quotes' You may like to have	
Look at other books for Ideas	
If you want to have Illustrations/Diagrams get them organised beforehand - hiring people via Elance is usually the cheapest	
Bring Along	
Your Iphone or Phone with a Voice Recorder App	
Laptop and all Chargers you may need	
Notebook, 4 Colour Pen, Highlighters	
All Your Notes	
Can Do Attitute - Ready to Play at 100%	

First point; be clear on your purpose for the book. What do I mean by purpose? Why are you writing this book? Who are you writing it for? Be clear on your target market and their problem. The purpose of your book; are you writing the book so that you make millions of dollars from book sales, or are you writing your book so that you can establish yourself as a credible expert in your market and in your niche?

In general terms to sell millions of books is an unrealistic expectation. If you're fairly new and unknown, I'm not saying it's not going to happen but you have to be realistic. I have sold more of my first book in the last 12 months than I did when it first came out.

Why is that? It's because more people know me and more people follow me and they're interested in reading the things that I have written. Remember, books are timeless, so as your credibility and expertise and positioning increases, your book sales are likely to increase.

What this would suggest is you create an initial purpose and intention around using your book as that entry to your sales funnel. We will discuss the sales funnel later in the book or the book can be that tool that will enable you to gain more trust and credibility in the marketplace. So I want you to ask yourself and then tick this part of the checklist so you're fully clear on it.

Secondly, be clear on your target market and their problem. After all, every book that's out there is solving a specific problem. What problem are you solving? Who is the person, who is that ideal target market that you're trying to attract? Being everything to everyone is going to result in you being nothing to no one. Choose a target market if you don't already have it that is going to be narrow, but deep. There's a saying 'an inch wide and a mile deep.' Even people in hairdressers when I would ask them "Who are you looking for as a client?" and they'd say, "Oh anyone with hair!" Now that is not a target market.

A target market would be a hairdresser that specialises in making blondes look fabulous. So her niche would be in the niche of colour, however she's even further niched in assisting blonde haired ladies or men into being or having their blonde colour appear amazing and fabulous. When you're thinking about your business and what your book is going to stand for, who is this target market and can you actually picture the person in your mind? You should be able to picture a single person. What their age is, what their occupation is, do they have a family, where do they live, what socio-economic status do they belong to and what are their secret desires. How are you going to deliver what they want in terms of your book and how will you give them what they need.

The next thing is to come up with a book title and have a few options, so that you can ask your family, friends, maybe even clients that you're currently working with what they like best. We'll talk more about this a little bit later on around how to come up with 'sexy' book titles, as I like to call them and market it exactly like your target market wants.

The next step of the pre-48 Hour Author checklist is that you want to have all your chapters and 'sexy' names for them outlined. What I always encourage people to do is first of all outline everything that they want to teach people within their book and then we would go through and structure the book in terms of what order things would appear. Then we give those chapters 'sexy' names.

'Sexy' names has been my thing that I often teach people so that they can distinguish between marketing and actually delivering what people need, because there are two different hats that we need to put on when we're delivering a service. When we've already sold it versus pre-sales in terms of our marketing. Prior to the weekend, you've got to have all of these things done and most importantly, this is the most crucial thing, is that you will need to have your chapters unpacked.

Chapter 3 will be the system on how to unpack your chapters so we'll discuss that in a lot of detail there.

You want to plan for your introduction and afterword. So again, just like your chapters being unpacked, your introduction and your afterword would be just an additional section within your book that you might want to write some notes about in terms of what you will say in these areas.

It might be the story behind why you created this book as an intro toward each of the chapters and the afterword I like to think of it as a bit of a pep talk to encourage people to go back through the book and take the actions that you have suggested throughout the chapters which you will notice that's exactly what I will do in my afterword.

Some people also come up and get someone to write a forward within their book and that could be an expert that's related within the area or the niche that you're writing for and they might then add say 1-2,000 words as a forward. So that's an option there for you. They might need to read your book first before they wish to contribute their name to it so keep that in mind.

I generally don't do them in my books, but I have had authors that I have mentored through my programs that have chosen to get a person to write a foreword for them.

Other things in terms of logistics that you would need to think about at pre-weekend time is around the design of your book cover. Think about the topic and what you would want to put on your book cover. My recommendation is if you are the business and generally at the end of the day, people buy people. If you want to be seen as a credible expert, you want to be putting yourself on the cover especially if you're in the industry as a coach, trainer, or a facilitator, you need to become the face of what you do and you need to be recognisable.

As you can see, from the cover of my book, I'm on my book and I thought about the design of what I wanted on the cover prior to me writing the book. I had this idea of holding up lots of books and having this to illustrate what the book was about. So think about the design of your book cover and when you have thought of your title at the same time you can send out those ideas to your family, friends and colleagues, and you can gain some feedback.

Any feedback is great feedback, because they might come up with something that you just haven't thought of. If you hear something that is not what you want to hear, or that you don't like, or perhaps you think it's a bit harsh and puts you off, just take it as feedback.

In life there's this other success principle; there's no failure, only feedback! Not everyone is going to have the exact same opinion. People are going to come from all sorts of different angles. When I promoted my book cover and asked people for ideas once I posted it up, there was some people that said, "Oh that clock on the front of your book looks a bit dated." However my perception was that books are timeless; so it just depends on the angle that you look at things.

That's what you're looking for when you ask for feedback. You might have those blinkers on and look at it from one angle yet another person sees it at another perspective. At the end of the day though, you need to be empowered enough to say, "If that's what I like and that's what I want, I will go with that. Thank you for the feedback!" and move on and do the things that you make a decision on doing.

So that's the book cover. The next thing is to collect some testimonials from past clients. Social proof nowadays is super important when it comes to people building trust with you before they know you. Often we see within books, people have testimonials of people having read their book however this doesn't always have to be the case if you want to get your book out quickly as fast as what we teach within this system. What you can do instead is get some testimonials around awesome work that you have done for past clients. So I normally collect around ten of these, pick out the best sentences within them, because you don't want to make them too long. Keep your testimonials to 3 to a maximum 5 sentences and place them to the very front of your manuscript when you hand it over to the publisher.

These are all the bits and pieces that you just need to collate and have in a file on your computer so that when you're ready after the weekend to send off your recordings of your book to a transcriptionist. When all of this comes back you're ready to actually cut and paste everything into one big manuscript and off it goes to the publisher.

Another thing to think about, because this is something that I didn't think of, is a dedication for my book, for my *Ninja Couch Marketing* book that I wrote with my fellow partner of that particular business, Donna Brown. I would encourage you to think about whom you want to dedicate and the reason for the dedication. Is it your family? Friends? Mum? Dad? Or someone that has made a difference in your life. It generally goes for one or two sentences and would be placed before the contents of your book. It's something that often can be omitted by people, so that's why you have this checklist so you can tick it off when you have typed it up for yourself.

We have come up with your programs and offers that will go at the back. So obviously you're delivering amazing, valuable information and education to people through your book. The next thing is for you to let them know what else they can get from you and after all, if the purpose behind your book is to build your business, build your credibility as an expert, you do need to show people the next steps. It's often been said, if you wet people's appetite, they will get hungry for more. That is why having some enticing offers (sometimes they could be free offers or if you run training programs or you offer any other types of services or packages) is important. I would suggest that you come up with them or if you already have them, to have them planned so you can drop them in the back of the book for people to seek out more information and to find out a little bit more about you and your business.

Then you want to write your bio. Your bio is the section called About the Author and this normally goes for about a page or two within a book, so you can give them a little bit of a story of your life or any professional accreditation that you have. You can keep it as casual as you want or as professional as you want. It's really up to you and the person that you are. This is where you also have to ensure that you do have a nice professional headshot that you could add of yourself if you are not using it on the cover.

I would generally recommend that you could even organise yourself a photo shoot prior to the weekend and have a book cover mocked up even before you have gone away. That way you can be ready to start promoting and doing your marketing as soon as you have a little mock-up of the 3D picture of your book cover which I will explain a little bit later on how to organise for yourself. A photo of your head shot as well as what ideas you have for your book cover would be something that you would need for the bio section and I'd like for you to do this prior to the weekend.

The next thing is to do the synopsis or the little blurb that will go at the back of the book. This is to really entice people to want to then go through and read the book. What we're looking for in the blurb is the use of a lot of hypnotic language, selling people what they want. The cover of the book is truly about selling the target market what they want so that you can have the opportunity to give them what they need. This is where I was talking about the book name and the chapter titles, because there's a difference between what people want and what people need.

Generally what people want in almost any business to any solution to any problem in general terms is they want it to be easy, fast, simple, they want it step by step. They want a system. They want more time, they want more money and they want more freedom. So in regards to that, I mean just reflect back on any book title, not just my book title, but have a look at the books on your shelf. They're selling you what you want.

I know Brad Sugar has the whole series of business books called *Instant Cash Flow, Instant Systems, Instant Leads*. Those titles are selling you that idea of quick and fast, but when you start reading them it's not so instant. You do need to take a certain action to generate what he's teaching right there and as you can see also, as you've been reading this book, there are certain steps you have to follow through. It is possible to write your book within 48 hours, there is however a bit of preparation and after work to bring it into reality. That long arduous task of typing out a book is seriously short cut so you can actually focus on the fun stuff.

Selling people what they want needs to go into the blurb or the synopsis at the back of the book using really hypnotic language. If you don't know what hypnotic phrases and words are, go Google them and you will easily find thousands upon thousands of them.

The next thing is I love quotes in books so I do highly encourage you to think about starting off your chapters with quotes. Having a secondary quote there and perhaps maybe even coming up with some illustrations around some quotes. In my first book I did quotes for each chapter and I got an illustrator that I hired to come up with little images to illustrate the meaning behind that quote. And you can really cheaply do this by hiring someone, by Elance.com and outsourcing it. For about 11 illustrations I paid about $80 and it's not too different nowadays. Don't think that publishing your own book needs to cost thousands upon thousands of dollars with all these professional things that you can get done nowadays for really next to nothing. Think about diagrams. Diagrams that you may have within your chapters or appendices so you want to have them prepared and organised beforehand.

Definitely have a look through any other looks for how they're laid out so you can start getting some ideas of what you might like to have within your book. It's really fun and this whole process is just putting the pieces of the puzzle together.

For the weekend you need to remember to bring along some tools. Your phone, if you have an iPhone or a smart phone or even a laptop you can record on. Right now I'm recording straight onto my laptop via a program called Audacity. Basically I convert the file into a wav file or an mp3, however you like to record as long as the person who's transcribing it can hear it and press play then that's cool.

What you do is you put your files in the Dropbox folder and you share it with your transcriptionist. Ensure that you take away your phones and your chargers; take any highlighters, pens that you might like to highlight specific things with in your notes and definitely take all of your chapter unpack notes, that are on your checklist and most importantly your 'can do attitude'! Be ready to play at 100% when you rock up for your 48 Hour Author Weekend.

Lastly within this chapter what I wanted to address is the few "what ifs" that come up. This is what has happened with me prior to hosting the weekend. People start to get overwhelmed and some have done more of the checklist and some have done less. Often it's like what if I ran out of time? So, is it crucial to complete the full checklist prior to the weekend? I would say, no it's not crucial! It's handy though if you do and it will make everything post the weekend a lot more fun and effortless and you can just focus on the marketing aspect of the book. But if you run out of time, the most crucial thing that you must complete are the chapter unpacks. The other things you can actually do while the publisher is working through your book, although you should be focusing on your marketing as I said as much as possible, post the weekend.

But your chapter unpacks (your notes for what you want to say in each chapter) just like I'm doing right now. I have one page of notes in front of me and I'm just talking as if I'm delivering a workshop. Those are the things that are the most crucial things to know. No you don't need to have everything absolutely completed, but the crucial thing is to have your chapters unpacked.

Other things that people come up with are *what if others are slowing me down?* Meaning other people in terms of transcriptionists or people that are doing illustrations for you, people that you're outsourcing work to. One of my answers to that would be do your best to communicate patiently or promptly. Always leave yourself a buffer of time when you're not relying on a deadline and then if you can't explain something to someone as something visual, draw it, send them a picture of it as to what you mean and generally people will do a good job. Definitely when you're outsourcing and dealing with people all over the world, really clear communication and patience must be practiced in inserting that buffer, because things can pop up. For example when I was writing The *7 Ultimate Secrets to Weight Loss*, the illustrator's mum unfortunately passed away and she didn't communicate that with me and I didn't hear from her for about three weeks. However I stayed calm, I emailed her a couple of times every week and finally she did come back to me.

Had I known I would not have emailed her and waited until she was ready or maybe I would have moved it across to someone else. Unfortunately things like that can happen so do practice patience and sometimes it can be something that's going on, on the other end that you may not be aware of.

If you do get stuck on some of these things, ask for help. Success is not a solo act; so do ask for help, even if someone's not a professional. People are generally happy to brainstorm with you and give you ideas, but definitely a professional would be someone who can point you in the right direction and get you unstuck as quickly as possible.

So go forth and print off or copy the pre-weekend checklist and start ticking things off as you're preparing yourself to go to the 48 Hour Author Weekend that you will plan for yourself.

Chapter 3

Ultimate Chapter Unpack System

A lot of people get stuck on where to begin and how to correctly organise the information that is in their heads. Many people I come across tell me, "Oh, I have so much knowledge around this particular area and that particular area; I just don't know how to collate everything together so that it's in a nice orderly way so I could present it to someone as a step by step system." As I'm writing this book this is what I'm delivering to you, a nice organised step-by-step system so you can follow it and action it to make sure your book becomes a reality within 48 hours.

Within this chapter I'm really going to teach you how to go about unpacking each of your chapters so that they do come across in an organised way and make sure that they are customised to all the sorts of personalities. What I want to give you is a step-by-step system for developing the content of your chapters that will appeal to many personalities, as it will cover the questions that may arise in your reader's mind.

This is a really easy format to follow and think of it as if you're delivering a mini-workshop, because really this way you can leverage the content that you have written for your book to run your mini-workshops or bigger workshops at the back end of doing this exercise.

This really will allow you to properly prepare to ensure that you have that 48 Hour Weekend success. The best bit of it is you're unlikely to get writer's block and have this picture for every chapter that will be really, really easy to follow. Normally what I say to all my authors that I mentor is to ensure that they use about one page per chapter to unpack all of their different ideas for what will go into each particular section.

As we go along I'll give you an example from one of my authors who came along to one of the weekends and how we went about doing that. I actually spend a couple of hours with each author before the weekend to help them get started on their chapter unpacks to ensure that they have created a sexy outline for their book and then to give them an idea on how to do one chapter for themselves and then to go ahead and unpack the rest of the chapters. The system that I teach people in terms of unpacking their chapters is called the *format system*.

I learnt this format of structuring workshops and even written materials through the educational institution where I did my coaching qualifications and it is one of the ways out there that is used to structure presentations and written material. In this case we're structuring each of the chapters of the book.

The format system has four different components that are the why, what, how and what if. Just to explain what each section is, so when you start up a chapter, we need to build the compelling reason why people should continue reading. Just as you may have noticed at the beginning of this particular chapter, I told you about it being a step by step system for developing the content of your chapters, that it's an easy format, it allows you to properly prepare for your 48-hour weekend success and it removes the dreaded writer's block experience. I gave you a lot of reasons why you need to continue reading. This is the same when you're thinking about your own chapters and what is the reason why or what are the benefits behind what you're about to deliver to a person. Let me take you through one of my authors, Russell Scott, who is also featured at the back of this book in the bonus chapter where I interview him on his experience. His book is called *Free Time*. When we sat down to unpack his chapters, I found out the purpose for him writing the book and who was the target market. What did this target market specifically want, because as we said earlier in the book there are two different things when we think about our target market.

It's what they actually want, that magic bullet, that quick fix, that step by step system, but what they actually need is the steps and all the content that you would deliver and the steps that it takes to achieve whatever it is that you're teaching them, which usually is not that quick a magic bullet as we have mentioned before.

With Russell's book we decided to go ahead with 12 chapters. I said to him, 'if you are going to teach people how to be more productive and have more free time so they can enjoy their lives and families, what are the things that they would need to know about? So give me all the boring titles that you would deliver, because obviously if we wrote a book on goal-setting and prioritising and systems and planning a lot of people wouldn't want to pick it up.'

So with Russell we came up with topics in boring terms and this is what I encourage you to do with yourself as well. Come up with a boring way that you want to teach people, so if it is planning, if it is distractions, if it is prioritising and goal-setting and mindset and planning and scheduling, write those down. Write all of the different topics that you want to go in with more detail. What happened is then we thought about what are the sexy names behind these topics. For example 'Goal setting' turned into 'Future destination'.

Now that sounds a lot more enticing and it focuses on their future, which everyone is curious about. One of the other topics he had was around prioritising, so rather than calling that particular section 'Prioritising', we named it 'Multiply Time', because it was a really cool name, that's what people want. They need to prioritise, but they want to multiply the time that they have. One other example would be the one around planning and scheduling and we call this particular chapter 'Digital Analogue'. They're all interesting and sexy names that will spark a curiosity in the reader.

Once we have done that, I also encouraged him to order each of these chapters in the order that he would teach people his strategies. This would then become the order of the chapters. Then we went back and brainstormed a little bit more around of the book name, called 'Free Time'. We thought a subtitle would be great, 'Business Time Lord Secrets Revealed'. This fits his brand 'Business Time Lord' and Secrets Revealed are hypnotic words again. It will spark interest within potential purchasers to want to buy his book.

The next thing I did with Russell and I'm giving this example so you follow this process for yourself, I said, 'Which one of these chapters would you like me to help you unpack so we can see how you go about doing this?' By the way guys Russell helped me out to put together an actual template you can use and I've put this in the appendices so you can photocopy it for yourself and you can use and unpack each of your chapters which was really handy and we will continue to use that in our future weekends with the upcoming authors.

Russell chose that we would unpack the very first chapter which was 'Future destination' and that was all about what is the person's 'Why' around them having a purpose and an outcome. So then I asked Russell, 'So in terms of having a purpose and outcome and a why, what are the benefits behind someone knowing these things for themselves and their business?' His target market was business owners who are very short on time and they lack having that effective productivity, so some of the things were the benefits behind knowing your why, purpose and outcome are that it makes your decision making easier. It does save you time and money. It gives you more clarity and direction in your business and your life. You become a better leader and also you have more sustainable energy.

What I did is encourage him to come up with five different benefits within the why section and that is exactly the same thing that I would say to you guys is have the minimum of five different benefits around your why section.

When you start recording your book just like I have, you would tie that into sentences and lock it in as if it's a paragraph, rather than having dot points. That doesn't stop you from having bullet points in terms of listing all the benefits, but sometimes it does flow a lot better if you actually say it into a paragraph as if you're telling someone a story. I said to him to think about some metaphors and statistics or contrasts that you can use to illustrate the benefits behind listening/reading this particular section.

I suggested he share the statistic that only 2-3% of people actually goal-set. If you do have some goal setting within that particular section, so knowing your outcome. Share that shocking statistic or give people the awareness as to what's going on around them. Then that's where we left that section and then we moved onto the 'what' section. For the 'what' section I suggested to simply define what having a purpose is and an outcome and how could someone go about discovering their 'Why'. So what is it? The 'what' section is very short? It's just a definition in terms of what you will be teaching someone within this chapter.

So for him it was: *I will teach you within this chapter how to define your 'Why' and how to go about discovering what your purpose is and how to plan out your outcomes that you want to achieve*. Then there was the 'how' section. This is where the bulk of your chapters will lie and this is about giving people the steps they need to follow in order to have success within the section that you're teaching them.

Number one Russell said was to get to the person's 'Why'. I would ask him or her the question, why did you start your business? Explore that with the individual in more detail. Then I said to him, could you think of a story where you have spoken to someone about this and what their answer was and what was the example? People learn through stories, so if he can put in as many stories and metaphors within the how section or even in your why section behind what you're teaching people, then they will learn a lot better and relate it back to their situational life and businesses.

So that's what he did. He came up with the story and he decided that is what he would put in that chapter and then I said well how else would you teach people about their outcome and purpose? The next question I would ask, he said, is for what purpose? Around that, I would give a story where a business owner posed this question to arrive at their highest purpose for doing what they're doing. Then the third bit within this particular section was that he would refer to the book, *Start with Why*, by Simon Senec, which I highly recommend that you guys get out and read because it is very important for all of us as business owners to really know our intrinsic 'Why' for the success that we want in our lives and businesses. This was going to be tied in in terms of discovering what their childhood games were, and perhaps how our whys intertwined between what we used to love doing as children and what our circumstances within our lives at that point in time were.

So that tied off the 'how' section so as you can see there was a lot of stories and examples he was going to share with that and as I'm telling you this story right now, I'm doing the same thing for you. I'm giving you Russell's examples so that you can then model that and then understand how to go about unpacking your chapters. Then comes the 'what if' section.

The 'what if' section is a very important section where you will need to address certain concerns and objections that people may come up with, following the steps that you have given them within that particular chapter. I simply said to Russell that you could call this the 'what if' section if you wanted to, or you can speak it out through your presentation and address those objections in a conversational way.

We came up with three questions that people may come up with:

1. What if my purpose doesn't reveal itself after doing these questions and exercises?
2. What if my purpose has changed?
3. What if my purpose doesn't seem achievable?

Then Russell would answer those questions and give people the explanation they need.

Then he would work through all of that and what he would do (this is how this happens in just 48 hours) is outline in one page what he needs to cover. When we go to the weekend, or you take yourself to that weekend, you pull out your page for chapter one, for whichever chapter you're doing, and then you start dictating it. You start talking and developing the stories and just figuring it out. Right now why I'm doing it freely. This is why it's important to have language around your expertise and I also encourage you to have practice before going on your way.

I recorded chapter 1 of this book and I really wasn't in the zone and I decided to rerecord it. Sometimes that may happen with you as well and you might want to start again.

If you do get stuck I suggest just pause the recording, regroup yourself, visualise yourself as if you're in a room full of paying clients attending your workshop and you're wanting to do your best to get your point across and really explain what it is that you're wanting to teach them.

Here's my 'what if' section within this particular chapter and that is, people often ask me, can I use different formats or a different structure system to come up with my chapters? To that I would say of course, whatever you have that will allow you to deliver your content in an organised way, by all means use it. Be consistent and make sure that you insert a lot of stories, examples, case studies, have statistics if you can find them because they really back up what you're saying. Discuss it with other people, because they will learn best through your stories and your metaphors.

Sometimes you may not like the way we have presented in the appendices the unpacking template of the chapters, so what you might want to do is mind-map what you want to present. You might want to come up with a PowerPoint presentation so then truly pretend like you're delivering a workshop and for some of my chapters I'll be doing exactly that because the content I have is previously prepared and delivered in workshops.

You might like to just write it down. I just like doing why, what, how, what if, on one piece of paper and then inserting the stories and metaphors in that piece of paper and then starting to deliver it. I can do both in PowerPoint. Mind mapping doesn't necessarily work for me but it may for you.

Then another question that comes up is, *what if I get stuck and don't know how to unpack my chapters and for the topics that I have selected?* Then I would say do some research or seek some professional advice. Is there some mentor that can actually assist you to extract this from you?

I understand that when you're doing this for the first time it can be challenging. That's why having someone by your side for a couple of hours, the way I do it for my own clients is going to be helpful enough to get you going and just think of the value in that for long term, when it comes up to doing more and more chapters in work that you want to do for future programs and for future, not just programs, but future books and the like.

That is the Ultimate Chapter Unpack System. It really takes about probably 20 minutes to 30 minutes for you to focus on in terms of unpacking each of your chapters. Nowadays I can sit down and do three chapters in half an hour. I would suggest not sitting down and doing them all at once. Maybe do 1-2 each time you sit down because I don't want you to get complacent, I don't want you to do your unpacking half assed and get bored with it! Do 1, or 2 at the most and then walk away, come back to it fresh and excited to be doing it next time around.

Print off your pieces of paper, I find it's easier when I'm holding my pieces of paper and speaking into my computer or iPhone and recording them. By all means take a break, do a bit of visualisation before you start dictating your chapters. Pretend that there's an audience in front of you and I'm sure you will come through with an amazing content for your book. Once you get it back from your transcriptionist, it will be amazing value and just so well written, because speaking something out versus typing it out gives you a different voice. Often times people have told me that it's a lot easier to read the conversational tone of something that has been transcribed from spoken word, rather than the written and typed out form of delivering when it comes to writing.

So good luck and for any questions, you're more than welcome to contact us and ask for assistance or further information.

Chapter 4

Business Leverage from Your Book

As discussed in previous chapters, the purpose behind writing a book when you're new in business should definitely be to establish yourself as a credible expert and really position yourself as a go-to person within your niche. Using your book should be the start of your sales funnel and if you don't know what that is I'll explain it a bit further on in this chapter.

The point is to grow your business; to use the book as leverage and to get people to come along and experience your products and services. Whatever it is that you want to offer and for more information about what you want to teach in your book. It's truly important if you wet someone's appetite you also have the next steps available for them, because, *guess what?* If you don't offer those next steps, they will go out looking and researching to discover who has further information in terms of what you are speaking about.

It's a fantastic way to up sell to higher end programs with your book and to back up your expertise. Additionally, your book ends up being a very powerful marketing tool, because people can end up sharing it with their friends. They'll end up noticing it even just sitting around. People don't tend to throw out books so it could be a great marketing tool for many, many years to come.

Within this chapter I want to teach you how to create your own table of value for your business and truly to explain how it works for the most successful entrepreneurs out there. That way you can also sell those high-end products and services that you have to offer at the back end of your book.

Here I just want to show you one of my old tables of value, which I used to use in my Ultimate Weight-Loss Business.

Ultimate weight loss – mentoring packages

What's included	Value	Discover your patterns	Get your dream body	Live your dream lifestyle
One on one 1hr coaching conversations	$2197/mth	Unlimited for 3 mths*	Unlimited for 6 months*	Unlimited for 12 months*
Ultimate Weight Loss Webinar Attendance	$29/mth	Included	Included	Included
Lifetime Access To Members Area	$39/mth	Included	Included	Included
Success Book	$47	Included	Included	Included
Monthly Tips for Success	$57/mth	3 months	6 months	12 months
Unlimited Email support & Laser Coaching	$197/mth	Included	Included	Included
Weight Loss chart and Menu spreadsheet	$47	Included	Included	Included
Book "The 7 Ultimate Secrets To Weight Loss"	$30	Included	Included	Included
Heart Rate Monitor Watch	$90	Included	Included	Included
Modern Bathroom Scales	$97	Included	Included	Included
Key learning's Personalised Portfolio	$97/mth	-	6 months	12 months
Series of 5 Videos for a Healthy Diet	$497	-	Included	Included
2 goal setting sessions	$375	-	Included	Included
5 Audio Interviews with different fitness experts	$247	-	-	Included
Your Success Program (Lifestyle re-construct)	$8,997	-	-	Included
Total value		$7,751.00	$16,645.00	$41,349.00
Your Investment		$1,997.00	$3,497.00	$6,497.00
Total Saving		$5,754.00	$13,148.00	$34,852.00
Monthly payment plan option - first month to be paid prior to 1st session		$665/month	$582/month	$541/month

* Unlimited coaching sessions are subject to scheduling availability, 48 hours notice must be given prior to each session. Pay per session also available!

What you will notice from this particular table is that there is a mixture of tangibles and intangibles. What do I mean by that? Tangible assets are things that you give to a person; like manuals, books, or any other products that would combine with your services. This is very important if you are in a service-based business, because with service-based businesses what happens is we tend to sell our expertise, however it's very intangible. When someone invests, let's say, $5,000-$7000 into working with you or one of your programs, it's nice for them to walk away with something they can touch and feel.

At the end of the day that is the thing that will remove buyer's remorse and make them happy with the decision they made to do business with you. Just imagine a person investing that kind of money with you and they come home and their partner says to them all excitedly, "Oh, honey! Look at what I've invested in!" And the partner would generally say, "Oh, that's great! What do you get for it?" If they have something tangible to show for their investment, even though that's not where the true value is, the buyer's remorse will be less. They will have some evidence to prove that what they have invested in is of particular value.

What I want to teach you within this chapter is how you can combine tangibles within your business, even if you don't have them at the moment. How you can make those tangibles relevant to your business while you're writing your book, so that one day it will become one of your tangibles. As you can see from the table that I've put up before, the tangibles that I used to give away early on in my business were really not my own. It was a weight-loss business I thought, "What's relevant to weight loss?" So I would give people scales, a heart-rate monitor and a diary, which was obviously not my own, neither did I brand it.

Later on as my first book came out I wrote another program and lots of other mini products began changing for these. I started taking things out that were not mine and putting more of my intangible intellectual property assets that were.

For another client of mine, whose niche is a time-expert, we decided that while she was preparing her own personal tangible assets, to actually go on EBay and look up a nice clock that she could give her clients. It was something that we found that was worth $20, but it was a nice little gesture to symbolise the work that she would be doing with her clients.

Other things that you could potentially do if you're a coach or a trainer or someone that is assisting people with empowering and achieving certain goals, is that you can get them a kit of stationery. A kit of stationery, something you could call a "dream kit", where people can record different pictures and visualisations. It's really something that once again, you haven't taken the time to create, however it adds that perceived value to what you're doing with your client.

This is where I want to explain perceived values, so when you look at a table like on the previous pages, you can see that the total value is far more than the investment. Why is this? Well, many entrepreneurs put this out there and often people don't understand it – how can something be worth $10,000 and I'm only paying $2,000? Well, perceived value is not a calculation, but it is a feeling. The feeling can go both ways! The feeling can be in terms of the amount of time that the particular person has taken to bring about and study the information and collate it in a digested way as well as the amount of research that would be done. There's a value within that!

Secondly, this perceived value could be seen as what the value is in terms of what the information would do for the person who is investing in it, because it changes the person's life and business. If you are going to read this book and write your own book within the 48 Hour timeframe and get it out there, I can guarantee you will experience fantastic business success. In turn, what will this book then be valued to you? The value could be hundreds of thousands, if not millions of dollars, just because you've followed a system within a book you only paid about $30 for.

So, perceived values, what do you think your products and services will provide to the customer in terms of the results that they will experience, but also, how much time and effort have you invested around the research and implementation of what you're providing today?

What you want to do is work out what investment is a reasonable and fair exchange for people to pay you for what you will provide. Further down, I would highly encourage you to offer people payment plans, because truly it makes it a lot easier for people to commit when you can give them a broken down payment plan. If they need it further broken down, I'm always of the mind never to say no. Always to make it easy for people to invest with me and also to be fair and reasonable over whatever period of time you both commit to.

Another thing that's very important when you're putting together your table of value is to use that principle of making packages and your different levels of packages sexy! For example the "Discover Your Patterns" I offered at the beginning, that brings up curiosity and discover is a hypnotic word. Just earlier I was teaching you how to come up with your book title and outlines, this also applies for your packages, the items within your package table, that you're giving people. You're selling people what they want. That magic bullet, that quick fix and that system that people want. They like it neat and packaged up! Within it you know that you will be giving them what they need, which is obviously all the steps and the non-magic bullet, which is usually how we get to success. Everyone knows that there really are no short cuts!

Some other tips I want to share with you are around designing your packages. Avoid making them too cluttered. Most of you will know the 'KISS' principle, which stands for Keep It Simple Stupid! Please keep them with lots of value, but not too cluttered! There's another saying that I always explain to my own clients and that is a confused mind will always say no. So do keep it simple!

I encourage you to always revise and adjust your packages and offerings every 3-6 months to see if you are still happy with them and if there's room for improvement, go ahead and add extra things or remove things that are not relevant anymore. Throughout my time in business, I have changed what I have been offering time and time again, simply because it's become better and more improved and higher value. I encourage you to do that as well!

Do creative prizes when you feel that you are delivering more value and that your clients are starting to get their results a lot faster. Over a period of time, you will become more intuitive and you will be able to help people a lot faster in a problem that needs solving. Just think back, to a plumbing apprentice for example, when they start out, they will probably take an hour to change a washer on a tap. However, as time goes on, two months later, they might be doing it within half an hour and a year later they might be doing it within 5 minutes.

Same thing with any expert and any professional within any business, the longer you do it, the faster you become and therefore you can charge a more premium price. Very, very important to ensure that there is always fair exchange between yourself and your clients, so that they also feel good about the transaction and they're not feeling ripped off. You also feel that you've been paid fairly for the value that you have provided back to them.

Later on in the book, I will be sharing with you my 10 Easy Steps to Bust Your Money Limiting Beliefs. Because what I find within price increases in a lot of industry, a lot of people have these limitations. They have this money blueprint and not just in business, but people have it in their personal lives as well. It's as if, you have always generated $50,000 per year, you always tend to generate around that much. Not more, not less! It's this blueprint. There's a guy by the name of Harv T Ecker, who wrote the book *Secrets of the Millionaire Mind* and he talks about this money blueprint and is a very interesting book to read. I want to share with you my top ten easy steps to bust your money limiting beliefs, because I was in the same mindset for many, many years. My husband and I used to earn about $65,000 each per year and to break through that from an hourly rate that used to be $30 and to now $500 per hour. It's a complete mindset change and I want to share the examples and the strategies I have used to bust my own personal money-limiting beliefs. If you want to model that, by all means, I would love to do the same for you because the way you perceive the world and money will completely shift.

If you're not sure where to start, what I would suggest is to do a little bit of research using Google. After all, Google is your friend! Use it frequently when you need answers to your questions but what I would also suggest is to look at someone in your industry and have a look at their tables of value and model what they're doing well within your industry. Either model my table of value or make up one of your own.

And another question that always pops up is, "What if no one buys my high-end packages?" What I would always say is, every 3-6 months, always review, adjust and change what you're doing in the sales process. How are you saying things? Test and measure that and ask for feedback from a professional mentor or a consultant and also ask yourself, coming back, do you believe what you're selling is worth that much because if you don't believe it, you won't be able to sell it.

You need to be fully aligned with the value that you're delivering and the price that you're asking to get paid for your products and services.

Let's start bringing this all together. The whole purpose behind writing a book is to establish yourself as an expert and position yourself as the go-to person within your niche and your field of expertise. At the back-end of your book is the potential to leverage and get people through to your hiring programs. What I suggest that you do now is to come up with some ideas behind what you can put in the back of your book. Once someone has read your book, they would go to the About the Author section and then after that are other services or products by you.

In here, what I suggest you have is three different offerings. One may be something for free. Perhaps the person that has read your book may get something as a bonus. Go along to my website and pick yourself up a copy of this particular video recording, CD recording, whatever it is that you want to give away and continue that relationship with the person who has purchased your book. In that way, they end up on your database and you can continue communicating using e-mail marketing strategies because sometimes someone can buy your book, but not end up on your database.

They could refer people and say, "Hey, this author is really cool!" And they might look you up and join your database via your upcoming events or whatever it is that your business offerings are.

Another thing you can have at the back of the book is something that's a low entry level. Is there some kind of a membership that people can become part of? Could you create something like that? Even before you've published a book, maybe you can think ahead and perhaps create some low-cost membership that people can become part of and receive amazing value from you.

The third thing I would put in is your top-end packages. I wouldn't necessarily put any prices for your top-end packages, because these may change over time so you may just want to get people to contact you and discuss further if it is something that they're interested in.

When putting together these three different offerings at the back of the book, I highly encourage you to think of putting a little illustration, or pictures that indicate what that product or offering is. That it's not just written down as text so make it a bit more graphically and visually appealing and if you can't do it by yourself by all means outsource it to someone else.

This is something that I highly suggest you think about prior to the weekend and through the process of the publishing, just before the book obviously goes to print because these are the pages that need to be inserted at the back of the book.

Another idea is that you may have your workshop offerings, that you would be happy to speak at people's companies, or conduct certain workshops and organisations. Think about maybe having that and a contact phone number that people can get you through.

It really is important that there is something in this section of the book, because people are always curious, "What else have you done? What else do you do? What else do you offer?" If you are stuck for ideas, do look at other people's books. Buy people's books that are successful entrepreneurs, have written lots of books and just check out how they do it. A lot of them do a lot of promotion in terms of having calls to action throughout the book. Personally, I'm not a big fan of that, because I feel that people are selling to me all the time when I'm reading books like that!

However, that is something you could choose to do. Have a look around, go to a bookstore, have a look at your current books that you already have and model what you like and certainly, learning this by yourself, all of my books have been at the back. In the very first one I noticed I didn't put it there, which is cool. You live and you learn!

So the ultimate actions that you need to take as a result of reading this chapter is to come up with your offerings and packages which you've bundled up with tangible assets as well as intangible offerings. Build up that perceived value and really deliver an amazing product that will make people contact you once they've read your book.

Good luck and I'll see you in the next chapter!

Chapter 5

The Tools that Make Business Easy

Technology. Love it or hate it? It changes so fast and so many new tools and applications get brought out every single day, there's probably one every second that comes out. Some people find it really easy and effortless to use and they just get it! Then there are so many others who are petrified about technology. They would rather do anything else than go near a computer. I now have come across many, many people like this especially around social media.

Social media is one type of technology I have found a lot of people are very reserved and scared of. They don't know what to post. They're not sure if what they're saying is the right thing and really they have this whole apprehensive attitude towards it.

Now I will be talking about social media in a later chapter, but in this chapter, I really want to emphasise and give you some tools that you need, to make your business really easy and smooth, with the use of technology. Everything is awkward until it becomes easy.

So always remember that! Once you know how to use a techie tool, you will love it. You will save so much time and once you set it up, you can really do a lot of things you can set and forget, unless it's something you need to come back to and reuse. Using technology nowadays does make you look more professional and your business has this perception for people that it's much bigger than it actually is.

After all, I run my business from what I like to call my "girl cave" which is my 'office' downstairs in my house!

I have never had an official office and I have never had a business loan. I just made do with what we had at the time and bit-by-bit we built this empire of ours. It didn't happen overnight and it's still happening, however the perception of other people out there is that we have this big office building and staff that actually help us. But no! It is the use of these techie tools that I'm going to teach you that enables us to appear bigger than we are.

Also, if you love technology, you will be able to sell a whole lot more books a lot easier and quicker and therefore you will get your name out there a lot faster as well. The other thing is, without technology, we wouldn't be able to work with anyone in the world. I have people that I work with from other countries that I license to my programs and systems. You can spread your business internationally and this is the only way!

What we're going to talk about in this particular chapter is some tools and applications, some software and systems that will make running a business a breeze and really wow your customers every single time!

I do want to break it up into three different areas, so I'm going to talk to you about the marketing tools that you need, some administration tools, and then some payment tools. Oftentimes if you are fresh in business and a start-up, some of these things you may not have already implemented so I want to make you aware of them and then you can choose what you want to do with the information and then invest in these applications and tools.

Some may be free and some you may need to pay for as a one off cost and some have those monthly retainers that you pay over a period of time and you commit to or it could be just a month by month option.

So let's get cracking!

1: Marketing Tools

There are three different marketing tools that I want to tell you about and the first one and the most important one for any business is their customer-relationship management system. This is where you insert all of your contacts to your database. If people go to your website and put in their details to get something for free, they would get transferred across into your customer relationship management system (your database).

An example of systems that are out there and the most commonly used ones are Mail Chimp, Office Autopilot, Constant Contact, Send Pepper (the mini version of Office Autopilot that I have used since the beginning of my business). Then, while you're a little bit further advanced there is quite sophisticated customer relationship management systems called InfusionSoft. This is quite pricey in terms of investment and their monthly payment fees are quite high, however, it is a really automated marketing system and has the ability to manage a database in a very sophisticated way.

The one that a lot of people will also start off in is Mail Chimp, because it can be used for free and it does have template newsletters that you can send out. However, the option to set up auto-responders is not there until you start paying for it. The other options are Constant Contact and Send Pepper, which I have used and they cost around $30 per month which is quite reasonable.

These are essential to have in your business because it's really the engine room of where everything happens and I'm not sure if you've heard this saying before, BUT the money is in the list! Focus on building your database of the people who you meet through your website and your social media and as time goes on, it just gets bigger and bigger. When I started out, I started with all my family and friends, I told them what I was doing, I sent them this email and asked if you don't want to get any communication from me just unsubscribe, but I'm starting my business and you guys are my first lot of people who I'm going to be communicating with.

If you want to keep in touch with me receive my e-mails or remove yourself freely from the list! As time has gone on this has grown into thousands now and with good management and insuring that I'm also always in contact, definitely sending out a monthly newsletter, as well as lots of other e-mails that add value. A lot of value being added back into my database through education and then at times when I would post and offer, or let them know that something is coming up or a workshop, and this is really crucial to have, because when we get onto the chapter around your marketing, this is what we will utilise for you to be able to market and tell the people that are following you (and are part of your inner circle) what is happening.

The next marketing tool is around social media. There obviously are many different platforms like Facebook, LinkedIn, YouTube, Twitter and Pinterest and many other platforms. Hoot Suite is an excellent tool that helps you manage them and see them all at once.

There are free and paid versions depending on how sophisticated you want it, or how many platforms you are using. I haven't used it myself although I have heard other people use it. I like to do my social media personally and it has worked for me fantastically, however, if you want to automate things a lot more, I have had amazing feedback that this particular tool and application is the one of choice out there in the marketplace.

The last marketing tool I want to share with you, because I recently discovered it (I'm so excited about this application), is called Capture. It enables you to upload your videos from your iPhone or your iPad, straight into your YouTube channel. The beauty of the Capture App is that you can trim a bit from the start or end of the video and click "upload", enter the title of your video and off it goes. Then you can go into YouTube and type other things, because there's nothing more time-consuming than plugging your camera into your computer, getting your film onto your (if you have a Mac) iMovie or editing it out or whatever it is you want to do, including posting it on YouTube, there's a lot of steps right there.

If you recorded a video (we will talk about video a lot in an upcoming chapter), you just use the Capture App and off it goes!

I was recently in Europe for five weeks and my mum was my assistant videographer and she took over 40-50 videos and as we were on the go I wanted to upload them and keep them in my YouTube channel and keep them as unlisted, and as time went on I'd slowly release them and promote my business from awesome and wonderful locations.

2: Admin Tools

With admin there are a few things to be aware of and the number one thing I want nobody to suffer from is the loss of their files or the video recordings of anything they have on their computer. When a computer crashes and if you cannot recover your work, I can imagine it's the worst feeling in the world. It's never happened to me, however I have always had backups and systems so if anything happened to my computer, my laptop, anything that I use that I would be able to recover files that are very, very important in my business.

So there is obviously the cloud and with having the cloud there is a system out there called Dropbox (Dropbox.com is where you would go to invest in it) and it's your online hard drive! It is up in the cloud so you can access it from all your computers, your iPhone, your iPad, from any smart devices. This way you store everything on there and if you adjust it on one computer, it ends up being adjusted on all of your devices and you have one file that is the latest version and should any of your computers crash or stop working for any reason, you have your Dropbox up in the cloud.

The minimum investment – there is a free version however I do suggest being a business owner you go to that first level of payment, which is around the $100 mark for 12 months whereby you receive 100GB in the cloud in your Dropbox. There are more sophisticated levels but you'd upgrade to those as you need them. Starting off with the free Dropbox which is only 2GB is very low and you'll find that you'll fill it up very, very quickly.

The other thing, because you're obviously writing this book via recording, there is an application I use called Voice Box that you can upload to your smart phone and what this does is when you actually record your voice it syncs your file straight into your Dropbox. I'm currently doing it on my computer and I save it straight into my Dropbox, however if you wanted to walk around and record on your phone with some headphones, then do it on the Voice Box app which will sync your file straight into your Dropbox and you won't have to worry about connecting your phone and transferring files across.

The last thing for admin tools is obviously your accounting systems – so what will you use to manage your invoicing and reconciliations and all those tools? The most commonly used lately is Xero, QuickBooks, or even the good old MYOB. I personally use MYOB, however in the next year or two I'm planning to move across to Xero, as it's been highly recommended and a lot of amazing feedback from people using it, as well as accountants and bookkeepers, highly recommending this system.

So if you haven't started yet I'd suggest having you look at Xero for your business.

The last lot of tools that I want to share with you are your payment tools. So how will people pay you when they actually come across to do your programs or packages or buy more of your products? There's a few different ways nowadays. There are instant payments that you could take with your phones. With my bank, there is a particular app where you register as a merchant and you can just type in the person's Visa or Master Card and take that payment on the spot as if you had a handheld EFTPOS machine. I know that PayPal has this same type of set-up, so you could set it up through PayPal and have the option to take payments on the go.

Another thing that's an amazing application on the go is called Invoice to Go. You can actually invoice people from your phone and get them to pay right then and there and you provide them with an invoice instantly so have a look at that application, it is actually free.

And the last thing is if you have membership fees or monthly retainers where people need to pay each and every month is to set up some kind of a direct debit account. Here in Australia we have Easy Pay and I believe there are many other companies who actually provide this service. Generally you will be paying a certain percentage of the person's fees back to that company for providing you that service and doing those direct debits for you. The beauty of it is that it is set and forget and that you don't need to wait for people to pay your or you don't have to process payments yourself. A third party does it for you, while some companies even chase up people that may have failed payments or for any reason, so have a look around at what's available so you get the best fit for your business.

We've learned quite a few tools here that you can implement within your business and some are the basics around having things properly set up, so that you can generate the business as well as take your payments and manage your customers professionally and easily and protect yourself against any loss of files or computer crashes. There are a few questions that often pop up around this from people that I've mentored in the past and still currently, that is a lot of objections around paying fees, because they can add up when you start making serious money. What I would say to that is it's really part of business! It's totally tax-deductible and I would always ask the question, would you rather be paid and pay fees, or wait, ask and rely on others and potentially not get paid at all? When you weigh up those two, a lot of people don't feel uncomfortable about following people up for payments, having something set up and on auto-pilot that will work for you without you needing to focus on it and you can focus on what you're good at and then paying those fees is totally a good thing to do to save yourself headaches and having to chase people up.

If you're not sure how to use some of these tools that I have given you right here, do ask for help. People generally are willing to help other people. Is there someone you network with that is an expert with bookkeeping? I remember I was networking with a very good bookkeeper and she spent a couple of hours with me just showing me a few things around my computer on how to do my reconciliations properly. Then I paid her a little bit to train me a little bit further, and now I can do all my accounting and bookkeeping correctly and hand it across to my accountant at tax time without thinking whether I've done it right or not.

You would be surprised how keen others are to help out when you actually ask. Remember, success is not a solo act so please ask for help! The last thing I would often come up with is that it's time-consuming to learn all these systems. You really cannot afford to not spend that time, because it's more time-consuming not to learn them. Just imagine how many times you would have to do something manually or phone calls you need to make. If you want to send many emails and you're doing it all yourself instead of on autopilot, then it's really just the time invested. For some people it will be longer, for some shorter, but it's time well invested to learn technology and get used to it.

What I also believe happens is that you may not be techie at all but if you start looking at a few different systems and learning them, you may start to get how computer applications and software work, so the more systems that you learn, the more you have this intuitive knowing for the next one you actually come up to.

Some of them are completely different, but oftentimes the principles and foundations of the basics around using techie tools is very similar. I encourage you to spend that extra time or even invest in someone to teach you a little bit about the techie tools and all of a sudden you'll see that you start to pick up on a lot of other technology and related products a lot easier yourself.

So go ahead now, I encourage you to pick three of the tools I have shared with you. One from marketing, one from admin and one from payment tools and start to use them and go for it and learn them, because you really need to have all of this set up when people start buying your books and investing in your business.

Chapter 6

The Secret Behind the Weekend Away

Why go away? Why not stay at home and write your book for 48 hours? Because in our everyday environment it's hardly inspiring and what I figured out when I did this for the very first time was that there was way too many distractions at home. The environment that I was seeing every single day was not getting me in that creative mode.

Therefore, when I decided to do my first book in 48 hours I decided that I would book some accommodation in an idyllic location so that I could get away from those everyday surroundings and get those creative juices going.

This allowed me, and it should allow you to focus without distractions, especially if you're a parent and you have children running around the house all day. There is a purpose and intention when you create a weekend that's specifically for writing a book, you make that commitment and you're set for that weekend to go away and have that quiet time and to come back with a completed project.

You have committed to yourself, which means that you're more likely to follow through. The beauty of the date when you set that weekend, is that you have that deadline of when it's going to happen. I highly recommend that if you're going to undertake this 48 hour author weekend structure, you do it the way I have been teaching you throughout the book.

The other thing that you're committing to is your family. Those that you look after, say your children if you have them and support you on this journey to give you the time and space to get this book written.

In this particular chapter we're going to talk about what happens on the weekend and how to structure your weekend with some of the things I actually do. I take the authors away to get their books written in a group environment where they have some "teach" segments where we educate about the growth of the business through the book as well as the actual writing and recording sessions that they get done so the work is completed and the book is ready to be handed over to the transcriptionist straight after the weekend.

What I would suggest is that you hire accommodation somewhere scenic and that you surround yourself by nature and ensure that the place you hire out is somewhere quiet and relaxing. You do need to have that mindset of having your ideas flow and you being able to express yourself in the best way possible. Go away somewhere that is one or two hours away from home so that you don't get tired or stressed from the travel, because after all you have just those 48 hours.

It's very important before you go away on your weekend that you have that plan set and I have already taught you how to unpack your chapters and ensure that you have gone through your pre-weekend checklist.

Now it's about creating a timesheet for yourself at the weekend and at the back of the book I've put an example timesheet of how our weekends look like, so you can get an idea of how to structure this for yourself.

The importance of this timesheet is that you give yourself ample amount of breaks and different sorts of activities that you can do in between your recording sessions. Essentially when you are recording your chapters, if they are about half an hour long spoken chapters and you're doing 12 chapters with an introduction afterward, then you're really looking at about 7 hours. You can probably get that done in one day, but you might be exhausted and might get complacent about doing them. You might try doing everything at once and might get bored at some point and do it half arsed.

So take away some relaxing music that you can listen to and have a break. Take away something (like a book or look at podcasts) that you can educate yourself on for your business. Perhaps something on how to leverage your book, because that is what we do in our teach segments.

In these segments we educate the authors of how they can leverage their business via their book and this is the important part, whereby they learn the strategies and the marketing tools and they're given the systems around the business growth essentials when it comes to using it as a marketing too.

Come up with your own timesheet, yours will be different to what we do. However, you still need to have some kind of structure so that you follow through and you come back to doing the do, rather than slacking off and having too many breaks.

The other thing that I would recommend is to ensure that you pack all your techie essentials. Take away your power cords, your computer, your phone if you're going to record on your phone and I suggest taking away some earphones – if you can pop those into your ears and plug them into your phone or computer, generally the recording will come out a lot clearer. This will also cut out some outside noise, which may distract you while you are recording so you can truly be in the zone.

Ensure that if there is a microphone you need to pack and all your food. Make sure that you're taking away food that is nourishing and will keep you energised and light during the weekend. There's nothing worse than hitting that 3.30-itis and having your sugar levels drop and you not feeling like doing the work and doing the recording so you want to ensure that your energy levels are up and that you're having healthy snacks whenever you're starting to feel peckish.

I'm going to warn you, you are going to get very hungry when concentrating and doing a lot of work, even though you're not being physically active. From my experience being there on the weekend we were all pretty much starving in between meals because we were using up so much brain energy.

When you sit down and actually write your chapters I suggest that you record only two chapters in one hit and then have a break and do something different. Don't do it all at once, because it is a big task, you need to focus. You need to get your information as clearly as possible. You don't have as much cleaning up to do after the transcription process. My recommendation is to do a couple of chapters, go away and then do a couple more. You can do it within your own weekend really, you can do it all the way through. We had a time slot between 9-5 to fit in but this doesn't mean you can't get up early to space out your recording hours.

Surround yourself with inspiration. It might be helpful to have music to inspire. To help you relax or to really get you pumped up so that when you're recording you're really passionate about what you're saying. That will come through in your voice as you record. Mix it up, mix up the locations where you're recording, so record chapters in different locations to keep things fresh.

Go outside, stay in the bedroom, do it in the kitchen, mix up your locations so that you continue to be inspired and you're not stuck in one spot if there's an opportunity to do that. Whenever you draw a blank when you're recording, just pause the recording. Don't press stop, just pause it to regroup and then continue.

You want to stop recording once the chapter is over and then save that file as your chapter number. When I start my recordings, I normally visualise myself speaking in front of an audience, doing it workshop style. I know some other people may do it differently. Before, I spent a bit of time interviewing Russell, who's featured in Chapter 13 of this book and he said to me that he actually juggled before he started doing his recording and he gives us the answer to that in chapter 13 so you can read as to why he juggled and what he did!

People might do different things. You might pump up the music and jump around the room for five minutes. But really, just use something and do a routine before you start recording yourself. And pause! When you need to pause, just pause, have a look at your notes, then continue speaking.

So as I mentioned previously, aim to record around 20-30 minutes per chapter. So on average, if you are doing 12 chapters with an introduction and afterward that would take you to 40,000-45,000 words, which is a decent-sized book in terms of how it would look when it is printed. You're looking at about 150 pages in a formatted book form. Always record your chapters in a separate file so that it is easy to complete the handover to your transcriptionist and then it's also easy for you to collate it when it comes back to you.

It is very important when you hand over your manuscript to your publisher for editing, formatting and layout, it's important that you are submitting one file rather than 13-15 different files and that you're submitting them in the order that they would flow in the book. Don't worry too much about grammar or fixing up little tiny mistakes, this is the role of the editor with the publisher! They will go through your book and properly lay it out and format it, the important thing is that the content is there and it looks in the right structure for you.

Store your files in a Dropbox folder so that this is the type of folder that you will need to share directly with your transcriptionist, and then in turn your transcriptionist can send back your document files that you can then cut and paste and clean up in the same Dropbox folder. You will be sharing this particular folder until you guys are done working together.

If you get stuck, you may need to walk away and come back to the task at hand with renewed energy. That's another tip for you! Start doing some sections. It's usually a little bit more awkward when you're beginning with Chapter 1 or the introduction; it just feels a little bit funny to be speaking to yourself out of order.

However, once you get in the zone or the flow, trust that everything that needs to come out will come out. What some people did at the weekends that I have hosted is some of them just started recording short little five-minute sections and worked their way up to 20-30 minutes without any dramas and they were actually really excited that they could churn out so much content as they were going along. Once you get on a roll you just can't stop!

I started recording this book by doing my recordings on Friday and I'm doing a little bit each day, because I want to have that break and come back to it and spend an hour each day on it and I did it on Friday. Today is Tuesday and I'm already up to chapter 6, I've done chapter 13 so I've only really got another 6 chapters to do, as the introduction has been also been completed.

I have this feeling that by the time this weekend comes along it will be completed and I will have it done amongst all the other things I do in my life. Now would I rather have done it while going away on a wonderful weekend? Yes, of course! However, I've got a lot of travel planned and I can actually focus on this task at hand when I need to because all my chapters have been unpacked and I've just got to sit down and do a chapter here or there. Whenever I have some gaps to bring out this information for you.

You can do it in your everyday life. You don't always need to go away if that's not feasible for you. When you're doing it for the very first time, I strongly suggest that you do go away, because that's where you can really just focus on yourself, focus on this particular project and get it all done in that time and then go back and focus on growing your business and your marketing for your book. After all, this is my fourth book.

Some people, when they're stuck, would write a sentence or a paragraph to get them started. While they were reading that out it got them into the free flowing way of speaking about the specific topic. I thought that was a great idea, because I often sit down and wonder how I will open up this chapter. Sometimes, something doesn't come that's really insightful to grab your attention, however, if I had a sentence or a paragraph that I could just read out, that would get me into the flow.

So again, remember all of this is going to be awkward until it becomes easy. I can guarantee you, by the end of your Ultimate 48 hour Weekend you will be in the zone.

The difference between recording a book through having conversations such as this is that it actually turns out to be very easy to read. It's easy and simple and just imagine how many times you can replicate the process for any writing that you actually need to do whether it's an article, whether you have done a webinar, presentation or workshop, you can actually transcribe everything you've said in those formats and use it in multiple ways to create other programs and products.

A few concerns arise when people are coming up to the weekend and they get quite overwhelmed a few days beforehand. I wanted to share with you a few tips around this and my advice to overcome it. A lot of my authors before they come to the weekend get really overwhelmed around the prospect of having to do this within 48 hours. They say to me, "What if I don't finish the book on the weekend?" My answer to that is that it doesn't matter! At least you've given it a go and you went out there and you've done most of it. You would have gone into the routine and understand what it's like to be doing it. It's not the end of the world if you come home and spend 4-5 days finishing it off. The whole intention is that, yes, we would love every person to have 100% success at their Ultimate 48 Hour Weekend, however reality is that it's unrealistic and we're not going here for perfection.

If you do suffer from the perfectionist syndrome, I suggest that you give yourself a break and that you acknowledge yourself of the work that you have achieved over your Ultimate 48 Hour weekend and that you commit and promise yourself when you get home and over the coming week or two that you will complete the rest of your book and will hand that over to your transcriptionist.

The other concerns that come up is when people get worried and can't express themselves. They've got in their mind what they need to say, but they think they're going to 'uhm' and 'err' and not say things the way they will come up. My answer to that is that prior to the weekend you do a little bit of practice and I highly recommend that you look for any opportunity to speak in front of people. What that does is really build your muscle to become fluent.

I don't let participants come along to the weekend unless I have the certainty that they have some kind of speaking experience and that they have language around their expertise. If you don't have language and cannot explain or teach to another person, then you're not ready to do the Ultimate 48 Hour Weekend. You need to know your stuff and you need to have those personal experiences. This is how I'm speaking here without needing to stop. It's because I know what happened, I'm speaking from personal experience from what I've observed and what people have told me and also what I've delivered to people. It's coming as if I'm telling you a story.

Think about it that way as well. Rather than saying that you need to be very technical, how can you tell people a story that you can teach them with tips and strategies? You need to practice, get some speaking gigs, practice in front of your family, or practice by yourself if you have to! While you're practicing, record yourself and listen to yourself and find out if you have got it within you. Do you like the sound of what you're hearing as feedback? If you end up with an awesome recording, why not keep that for your book. You never know, before the weekend you might have practiced a bit and recorded some stuff that has come out awesome you can use that as part of your book because nothing is ever wasted. That's why I always say to people to record their workshops and webinars. Anything that you do, any speaking engagement, just keep recording everything because everything can be transcribed nowadays for low cost. On Elance or Odesk, you should be able to find someone to do it at the cost of around 30-60 cents a minute.

The last thing I want to address here is that a lot of people start feeling nervous and I feel like, "What if my book sucks?" Recently I came across a Nike ad on Facebook and it said, "Just do it! Even if you suck!" That has been my motto in my business since I started out, because at the point of time that you're writing your book, you're doing the best you can with the resources that you have available for you. You know what, your subsequent books, your second, your third, and your fourth (be careful if it comes a bit of an addiction!) will be better. You will be better because you have grown and learnt. When I look back at my first book, *The 7 Ultimate Secrets to Weight Loss*, it doesn't even have sexy subchapter titles! The title is hypnotic, but it doesn't have those sexy outlines. I didn't put my programs and packages at the end of the book. I didn't do any of those things that I recommend authors do nowadays because I didn't know.

You will always improve. The being comes in the doing. If you want to be an amazing author, do the do, write, and keep repeating things, because one day you will start bringing an amazing product and it doesn't matter if you suck because you are going to be in a very small exclusive group of people who have become an author. You have actually been brave enough to step up and stretch out of your comfort zone to do something different, to propel yourself in your business further.

Chapter 7

The Power of Video and Your Character

Recording videos and being in front of the camera is not a natural thing for a lot of people. However, in today's world, with so much international access, the only way to get to meet people and for them to meet the real you is via video. Get used to creating videos once you become an author, because when you have written that book you do become that go-to expert that people want to hear from.

And it's an amazing way to really leverage and increase the conversion, especially on your websites. It increases the optimisation of your website, because Google loves video and Google is connected to YouTube, therefore it will push up your website a lot higher. You build a lot more trust a lot quicker when you actually put videos out there and you can start to get a serious following of people who are connected with your message.

It does keep you being creative and thinking of awesome, funky ideas that you can put up for people to see. Your message has a lot more feeling within it, because you can express in your tone, with what you do, the body language that you show and people can really get that exact feeling for the person that you actually are behind the camera.

In this particular chapter I want to teach you a bit about recording your own videos and how to leverage them for your business. Video is something that I have been doing since day 1 and the last time I checked I had uploaded about 250 videos on my YouTube channel and that was kind of a surprise, because I hadn't thought I'd done many! I started doing videos about six months into my business and I can tell you, you can actually see for yourself if you go and visit my YouTube channel under Natasa Denman, and you go back to the really old videos from my first book, *The 7 Ultimate Secrets to Weight Loss*. Oh my goodness! I cringe now watching them, but if I hadn't gone through the process of doing those videos, I would have never gotten to a point where I can speak as eloquently and fluently and really become this one-take wonder that I am nowadays – or so my husband tells me that I am.

First of all though, I want to give you some of the tools that you need. Often people think they need professional set-ups and lighting and all that stuff but it's not like that nowadays! Yes, if you have got the cash flow you can organise a film crew and do some really professional videos, however at the end of the day, people like to deal with real people. As long as you've got your message and your personality there, the quality of the video is not all that important. Again, I want you to remove the need to be perfect. All you need is your smartphone, which would have a camera application in it or some sort of a video camera, if you are doing longer workshops. Obviously everything that you're doing and hosting when you're in front of people, I suggest that you record, because what happens is that it ends up being instant product creation and further content you could transcribe and have in future books or as part of ebooks that you want to create for yourself.

The camera that you want to use for longer workshops and trainings does need to have a couple of different features that are very important in this instance and one of them is to be good in low light situations. I use a Sony camera. It has a setting for low light situations called EXMOR. Another thing you want to ensure is that you have enough memory to take a full day's worth of training or recording. There are cameras now with in-built memory or memory sticks that you can purchase and put into them that could possibly record 6-7 days of straight training for you.

Those two are a couple of things to be aware of when investing in a proper camera for video trainings and workshops. You want to have a tripod, so you can set up your training camera, or that will hold your iPhone if you do not have someone else to hold your phone and take the video for you.

They can be purchased from EBay and you can even have ones that turn towards you and you can actually review it so you can do it yourself.

For editing of your videos, on Mac computers, I use iMovie and it's really easy to edit out any errors or snippets out of the video. It's also really easy to put a nice intro and exit and if you have a PC computer then you can use Windows Movie Maker or something of a similar sort, and they work very similarly, where you can insert your website, your name and do a little bit of editing.

If you don't know how to use these programs and you've had a bit of a play and you're still struggling, I suggest asking people around you, in your network. Who has had experience using it? I guarantee in half an hour of them showing tips and tricks and you taking some notes, you can also become a competent editor of short videos. If you need to edit out longer trainings and workshops, I suggest not wasting your time! Hire someone via Elance or Odesk and actually get him or her to edit it for you.

I recently had five days worth of training to edit out and what I did was to post the footage to Bulgaria and a guy over there edited five days into one-hour episodes for $50 per day. For $250 I saved myself weeks of work if I had been editing it myself and I could focus on the money-generating activity in my business.

When you're running training and workshops I suggest that you have your camera continuously plugged into the power, so the battery doesn't let you down and you stop recording halfway through.

That's pretty much all the tools that you need; iPhones are amazing for taking small videos. Often people ask me, what kind of a camera you use, your videos look so crisp and clear. They're surprised when I tell them I use my iPhone, it's a lot easier when you do that!

Also you want to consider using your phone for testimonials, because you don't want to be shoving a big camera in front of someone's face, because it makes them feel awkward. When you use a phone though, people are used to having pictures taken of them so it's not as scary as when you have a large video camera in someone's face!

So just remember when you're doing your own videos, you will improve as time goes on. Same as when we're talking about recording our chapters. It will be awkward in the beginning, but with the repetition and you doing your best you will improve. I want to share the story of those first videos I did, because it's a funny story! You won't imagine the lengths I went through to ensure that I came across fluently without any erms and errs! What I did (as I was so worried I would draw a blank or forget what I wanted to say and I would erm and err along the way) was write stuff out on a big cardboard sheet and read from it.

I tested that out and it did come across as if I was reading, so that didn't work!

Secondly, I looked up one of those programs that the newsreaders use; there are free ones on the Internet. I thought maybe I could use this and read through it! However, again it came across as if I was reading. The last solution I had, which was because I was being very resourceful, was to record my voice on a voice recorder. I plugged in the headphones (I have really long hair, I covered them so you wouldn't see that they were in my ear) and when my husband was recording me I was actually following my voice on the recorder, so that I looked like I was delivering the message and it was flawless. Problem was I sat very still and it wasn't very natural.

Well I nowadays look at those videos, and if you guys get a chance, go along to my YouTube channel, do have a look at the very first videos on *The 7 Ultimate Secrets to Weight Loss* book, there's about 12-13 of them and you will see that those videos I've recorded come across as okay, but there's a difference in my personality. It's a completely different energy, yet I did the best that I could with what I had at the time and that's what went out and that's what I used and I'm actually still proud of those videos because I can show them to you and just say that, "Look at how crap I was! How much I sucked!" It's okay to suck because you don't know you suck at the time; you know you're doing the best you can. Perhaps the videos that I'm doing right now suck, but ones that I'm doing in 2-3 years time, I will look back at the ones today and will actually think how much I've grown at the time.

The question I hear is, "What would you want to record videos for?" There's a few different areas where I would love for you to use video and get used to doing it regularly, because it's really important that people are continuing to meet you and see you. I take the opportunity when I go away on holidays to use the beautiful locations I'm in to record lots of videos for my business. At the end of the day, I am selling that lifestyle and it is about having that lifestyle through the business that I have built.

Often it will be in the snow, at the beaches, in wonderful historical locations because I do travel a lot and I enjoy a wonderful lifestyle because of my business. These are the perfect spots to do lovely videos, because people will be inspired by your message as well as enjoying watching them because of the scenery! So record videos!

Now that you have recorded your videos, where do you put them? Put 3-4 videos on your website; your videos shouldn't be any longer than three minutes, unless they are obviously a video of a webinar or training that you have done, where people sit and watch. However, the short ones that you would share on social media and that you would have on your website, I wouldn't make them any longer than three minutes and make a lot of them between 1-2 minutes long. People's attention span nowadays is quite short! They want the information, they want the tips or teaching and they want to get on with their life straight away.

You would most likely have a video on your 'home page' and your 'about us' page introducing yourself. Instead of people having to read through stacks of copy, I would have a video about your services, again talking through your services. Even on your 'contact us' page, usually I combine my 'contact us' page with the 'about us' page and then I introduce myself and point towards the bottom for people to fill out the contact form and get in touch with me.

Those are the areas I would have on the website, then I would utilise lots of video, lots of 1-3 minute videos via social media, maybe releasing 1-2 per week would be a good idea and sharing them around. Asking people that follow you to share them around if they think they have a valuable message, because then you get exposed a lot to a bigger group of people and people just start enjoying your message and sharing it with more and more people. That way you grow your brand and following!

Having a video for your book pre-release campaign is essential! People will get to meet the author behind the book. This video is the video that would go onto your pre-release sales website and where you will talk a bit about the book and encourage the audience to purchase the book, at your pre-release price.

Also, what I suggest within this video is to think about whether you could have an additional bonus offer, for when people pre-purchase your book at that early bird price. Think about an offer that they could maybe spend half an hour with you, could they get an additional recording? Could they get an additional video or resource that you have done? Something where you can add more value to the pre-release buyers who are buying the book before it's actually come out.

I would record videos as blog posts and actually sometimes the right blog post, sometimes pick them up as video. In this case you might want to make your videos a bit longer. Five to ten minutes of length is usually pretty cool for a blog post. Record videos to introduce yourself to people on whatever format you're using throughout all your social media. You can embed video into any of your presentations. I recently ran a webinar on the insider view of the 48 Hour Author Weekend and this is where I showed them around the house and a few of the bits and pieces that we were doing throughout the weekend and it turned out as a nice little video that I edited out and popped into that presentation.

You can collect testimonials as video, which is the most powerful way to actually collect testimonials, because they give people the real person behind the experience and the fact of the matter is once you have it on video, that means that you can transcribe it and have the written testimonial as well as the video so you have it in both formats.

The social proof behind video is second to none so make sure that you collect as many video testimonials as possible.

You can record all your workshops and training and webinars and upload them. You don't necessarily need to upload them and have them listed as 'public' in your YouTube channel or whatever platform you are using. To explain that, there are three different types of video on YouTube: private videos, unlisted videos and public video. What they mean is that the private one nobody will be able to see, just yourself! Unlisted ones can only be shared with people if you give them the link and the public ones can be searched by anyone all over the Internet where they can see who you are.

Ensure that you select the correct settings in terms of how you want to produce your video and who you want to deliver it to and give access to. Do share your videos, post your media, it's a powerful way to perform that goes hand in hand. YouTube, Twitter, LinkedIn and Facebook really do go hand in hand and your videos can get that much more viewers through sharing them on social media and encouraging your followers on social media to share your videos.

So once you have recorded yourself on whatever format video you're doing, whether it's a webinar or training or little tip video, ask yourself a few questions:

- Can I transcribe the material and provide this in another format? As we said, video can easily be transcribed so you can then have the written format of this.
- Can I create a series of DVDs that I can package up and sell as a program, a tangible program? This would result from you running workshops and training.
- Can I upload these online and provide them as an e-course? If you were to upload your training videos within an unlisted format, and create a playlist that is also unlisted, you can then share this particular playlist, just with the people that pay for this particular

e-course and then you can just share the link with them when they have submitted payment.

- I can add this to a membership area that I could ask for payment? Could you build a membership area where you could build your own inner circle whereby people get access to all the support videos, a lot of written mindset content, they get a live Q&A, unlimited e-mails etc. All those features that combine to create a package, so that they get access to all of our resources as well as getting specific customised answers to all their emails and questions.

Think about all of these areas that you could potentially leverage your video and make it an aim that you record a couple of videos every week. You don't have to do it at separate times; sometimes you might select one full day that's going to be your video-recording day. You actually go away for a couple of hours with your video person who's going to hold your camera and have all your topics listed on paper on what tips you want to teach people, what you want to record, and just record a full month's worth of video. You can then upload the videos as unlisted and then slowly release them and make them public as you are ready to release them each week, one or two at a time!

You don't have to be constantly recording video, you can have one day in the month, a couple of hours, which is going to be the time that you go away and you record them and then you slowly upload them all at once.

The last tip I'm going to share with you here is using the Capture app, which links up with your phone's videos, which means that you can upload your videos directly onto YouTube from your phone. This makes it very easy for you to get them up there as quickly as possible, rather than having to plug your phone into the computer, get them off your phone and upload them. There are a few steps involved if you're doing it through the computer, but if you can do it through the Capture application it's much easier. I've done it so many times. Recently I was in Europe and I did 40-50 videos and I couldn't think of anything worse than to do it the long way. When I discovered this app I got very excited and just began uploading everything with the title. All I had to do was write a proper description in my YouTube channel, but once it's up there you can really tweak and edit your video and you can also select the privacy setting, so I put them all as unlisted until I needed them.

In terms of writing descriptions for your video, I always encourage people, and this is what I learned from someone who's got over 2,000 videos on their YouTube channel, is that they always start and finish with the URL of your website. Starting with the http and your website address and finishing off with that with keywords inserted into the description and the headline of your video. What you name your video as well as your description settings are very important. Use keywords that people are going to be searching for in order to find the information that you provide.

Finally I just want to finish off this chapter; sharing some tips and some objections that come up with people. They say to me, what if I freeze when that camera comes on? Just keep going. Keep going because you can do amazing edits through iMovie or Windows Movie Maker that will eliminate any stuff-ups that you've done and you only release the good stuff. Even when people give you testimonials, if they stuff up or freeze up, just tell them to keep going. We will edit out anything that hasn't come across the way it should, we'll make you look fantastic. So even if you're stuck and need to think about something, just keep going. It can be tidied up and will come across really awesome.

Another thing is that people worry that their videos look amateur and unprofessional and as I said early in the chapter, it's not about being squeaky clean and perfect. It is about people seeing you as a real person, being able to relate to you and warm to you and to build that trust and relationship with you. That's what it's about and you will come across more professional, you will get better at doing them as long as you actually start doing them.

And if others are feeling weird giving you video testimonials, as I said, use your phone, use your hand-held camera, rather than a professional video camera that you would shove into their face and just keep encouraging them that you will not post a video of them until they've approved it and once you've done the edit on it.

If you've delivered amazing value to people they will be more than happy to give you a testimonial. They'd be jumping at the chance to give back in some way. Make video part of your marketing strategy. It is the way of the future; more and more people are doing it. People who are not using video are seriously missing out on an amazing opportunity to market themselves and their business.

As we're going to talk about in the pre-release campaign of your book, you will see how important video will be in this and how it will leverage your sales and get more people to start following you.

So all the best, go out there now you've read this chapter; why not give your first video a go!

Chapter 8

Pre Launch and Launch Smarts

In order for you to make back the initial investment of producing a book, it is important to implement a pre-launch campaign that will drive sales even before your book is physically in your hands. Driving sales to the pre-launch is important because you end up building a hungry crowd that is eager and keen on waiting for your book launch. You have the ability to pre-sell your book at a lower price, which means you would be able to cover the cost of your publishing.

With each one of my books that I've brought out, I have pre-sold enough copies to actually pay for the publishing costs, which is really rewarding and it means people are already getting excited about it.

You get to celebrate your journey through your pre-launch campaign with your nearest and dearest and your importance around getting your publicity in getting your book launch; something that will make you sell more books. Through this type of campaign, what you will also end up doing is building a community and tribe around you, who are following the updates as the book is nearing its launch.

In this particular chapter I wanted to teach you about how to run your own pre-launch campaign and a few tips around having a launch party once the book is ready to come out.

At the back of the book in the Appendices section is a spreadsheet for your pre-launch campaign and I'd like to take you through that. What

I'd love to do is tell you how to set up a pre-release website, so that you can capture those sales through your pre-launch campaign and then I would love to give you tips on how you can really leverage social media for your business.

The pre-launch campaign is very cheap. When you're running a pre-launch it's important that you initiate a few different activities, which will consist of some online and offline marketing for your upcoming book. Some of the offline happens while you go out networking. My tip to all the authors is to laminate a copy of the 3D widget of their book cover and then take that out and show people. Get them to get a sense and a feeling that this particular book is coming out and then have a call to action for people to pre-order your book prior its launch.

I would normally set up a pre-launch price at $5-10 cheaper than when the book launches. For example, if your book is going to sell for $30 once it comes out, maybe pre-sell it for $19.95 or $24.95. Ensure that you're obviously taking into account the postage costs. Normally if it's within your own country say it would be $5 postage and if you're posting internationally you might charge $10 for postage.

I would print off and laminate the sheet that will have the cover of your book and whenever you stand up at networking events to tell people about what you do and what's new and upcoming in your business, promote your book! You will be surprised how many people put their hands up to be one of the first ones to receive a copy of your book.

The others things to do at pre-launch contain a series of articles, videos, social media posts; all that's emails to your database. So if you have a look at the spreadsheet in the Appendices section, you will notice that I have put down "article, blog, YouTube video, Facebook and LinkedIn and Twitter Updates as well as emails to your database". What I encourage you to do (why I have put together a weekly spreadsheet) is a weekly activity to promote your upcoming book.

The aim would be to write one article or one blog each week that you can release. Record one YouTube video leading up to your launch of the book. Plan a 12-week pre-launch campaign. Your aim should be to write 12 articles, to record 12 YouTube videos, and to have lots of different posts on your social media platforms that will give people tips from inside the book.

Now if you don't have a lot of time, you might choose to select snippets from inside the chapters, to share as the article and blog and you could pull out 500-700 words, which would be a very small section, less than 10% of your chapter that you can actually share. This is how you save a bit of time and get people excited and want to keep reading.

With your YouTube videos, I would be making videos that are less than three minutes long and again you might choose if you have 12 chapters in the book, one key distinction or insight to be recorded that you would like to share from your chapters in your YouTube videos.

Set aside one day when you're going to sit down and record. Have someone help you out. If you don't have someone to hold your camera, purchase a tripod that will hold your camera, or if you can get someone to assist you and give you feedback, that would be a great way to spend a few hours in one day recording all 12 videos. What you do is then upload them to your YouTube channel and then only release them one at a time.

Decide with your spreadsheet, what will be your day when you will be releasing your pre-launch videos? Most of the time people will take action on Tuesdays, Wednesdays or Thursdays when it comes to business so I would suggest one of those days when you do your YouTube launch.

Articles and social media posts, definitely throughout the week is the time to really put that out there. In saying that, you have to remember when it comes to social media, that 90% of the time, you are actually adding value and educating people and giving them information that will help them out.

So the pitching should only occur 10% of the time! There's a fine line between you over-promoting and always talking about the book, so make sure that your content and social media is a mixture of adding value and humanising the content and sharing a bit about yourself and your life so that people can relate to you.

Therefore, your likeability and trustworthiness increases and then about 10% of the time, you would make an offer and pitch something. During this period, you are really building up the excitement and are adding a lot of value through the content that you will be delivering through the book and at the same time educating people and then, once a week having that call to action for people to pre-purchase your book.

In order to make those pre-purchases a reality, it's one thing to release the videos and articles, blogs and social media posts, however, you need a place where people can purchase your book. This is where your pre-release website (it can be just one single page that you get someone to create for you and integrate a shopping cart so people can purchase via credit card or their PayPal account) is essential to have, because it's important for people to be one click away from purchasing your book.

Here are eight things you need to consider when setting up your pre-release site for your book:

1. You must have your 3D picture of your book ready! This is something your publisher, or someone via Elance or Fiverr or Odesk can set up for you. Don't be too precious; you can have something

mocked up that's not going to be your final cover, from fairly early on so put that up there, just so people can have that sense of the tangible nature of your book. Once you get your proper cover, replace that. It's okay! It's just important to have that 3D picture.

2. You need to have written the about the author section. This should be around 100-150 words. It will be about you, why you decided to write the book and what your expertise is. You might want to share some of your qualifications. Make sure it's short, sharp and sexy as I would say. Make sure it makes you look credible and as the go-to expert.

3. You need your sexy blurb! Your sexy blurb appears on the back cover of your book. This is where you're selling people what they want and it's really getting them excited about looking inside the book. What would people want to see on the back of the book in order for them to want to read the rest of it? Ensure that you are selling them what they want. Selling them what they need is going to be easy, there's a promise of more time, more money, that it's the magic bullet solution so that they can be driven to want to read your book and get the step by step system. After all, as you're reading this book right now, you're getting all the steps. It's not so quick and simple, but it is a system and if you take those steps you will have success with it. After all we know there are no quick fixes in life. However, to buy into an idea, to buy into reading a book, we always look to invest in that quick fix.

4. Decide what price you will launch your book at and what you will sell it at pre-launch.

5. Record a pre-launch sales video that will appear on your pre-launch sales page. Within this video you might want to give people a certain bonus for pre-purchasing. You might give people a 15-minute laser conversation with you around a certain topic. You might give them a bonus video, a bonus audio. Think about what

kind of bonus or what kind of incentive would you offer people who actually pre-purchase your book at the pre-release price. This is really to entice them and increase the value behind what they're getting.

6. You need a headshot of yourself. Do have one professionally done. This will appear somewhere in the about the author section of your website or sales page and can be used on your cover if you decide to.
7. Make sure that you have PayPal set up so that the person who is designing your website can integrate it on your sales page so that when people buy it comes through straight to your PayPal account. This makes getting paid easy!
8. Choose the address of the book (the URL). Usually people choose their book name. So for example, when I was doing the pre-sales for this particular book, people went to ultimate48hour.com.au. Then the person who's creating your website will also provide you with hosting of that website or you can buy the hosting yourself.

These are the eight components that you need to bring about your pre-release website for your book sales page and to make sure that it's got all the components that you need, so that when you send people to the sales page, it's easy and simple for them to buy and to find out a lot more information.

With your video including the bonus offer, the last thing I want to say is that you want to ensure that you are selling people what they want. What's on the back of the book needs to mirror what you're going to say in that video. Get people anticipating that this is going to be the best book that they're ever going to read!

As the pre-launch comes to an end and your book is nearing its official release, you need to start planning for your launch party. Having a launch party is not about having an ego or something that people think is about showing off, it is about celebrating this big milestone and a project that you have now completed. Give yourself 4-6 weeks lead-in time, even a couple of months if you can, to really promote and get excited about coming along to your launch party. Invite everyone you know: family, friends, colleagues, networks, and everyone that has followed your journey. The best way to do this is through your social media platforms and keep reminding people in the lead up to your event. You need to organize a venue, and perhaps provide some drinks and nibbles for people. You don't have to go overboard and the last thing to remember is to make sure that you have a person there on the night that's going to take the book sales for you. You're going to be busy chatting with people and talking about your book, as well as signing copies. Ask a friend, or your partner, someone you trust, to take care of the sales of the book.

This way you can enjoy the signing sessions as well as talking to your fans and family and friends on the launch party night.

Another thing to consider, and that is if you have the cash flow, is you could invest in a publicity campaign. There are people out there and companies that provide publicity for a fee. What they will do on your behalf is to contact the media and pitch a story and an angle that would be of value to the media to bring out either in magazines, on the radio or on TV.

For example, for this particular book, I'm organizing a publicist and I'll be working with him over a three-month campaign.

One of my authors, Justin Fankhauser, author of *Confessions of a Locksmith*, hired the same person that I will be hiring. Within a month, he was on all the morning shows, in about five or six different magazines, and between 30-50 radio interviews. It's really been a whirlwind media campaign. It's really paid back tenfold in terms of the publicity that he's received.

Now publicity will not work for everyone. You have to have a really good angle that you can go in on with the media. What I strongly suggest is to discuss this with these professionals because they do it all of the time. If they do it honestly, they would be able to tell you if you've got an angle that you can pitch. Not every single one of my books had the angle needed, but I had a great feeling about this particular book with publicists and therefore we will go forth and do a campaign.

Always be prepared to take the risk. Be prepared that the money that you invest may not turn into anything back to you. Treat the experience as an experience and whatever you gain from it, even if it's just feedback, then it's a great learning experience. You learn how to do things differently. Consider having a publicity campaign for your book, if you've got the cash flow to invest and if you've been advised that would be a good idea.

Either way, even if you don't do a publicity campaign, you will strongly benefit from becoming an author. You will be leveraging your book or your business via your book in a much better way through other avenues.

A lot of people are busy and sometimes they get worried about not being able to have the time to complete all the bits of the pre-launch campaign. Really it doesn't take a lot of time. Same as the pre-preparation for the weekend, most of the weekend is what this entails. You could spend a couple of days, again six to ten hours really putting together all the different sections of what your pre-launch campaign will release. You could spend a couple of hours cutting out and pasting articles and blogs that you will have, so they're ready there on the side for you to post. You could spend 3-4 hours in one day doing all your videos and you can spend another 2-3 hours coming up with lots of different social media posts. You could even schedule them so you don't have to think about doing them again.

With planning, you can get yourself organized and get everything set up so you don't have to be doing this every single day. Think about doing it more effectively and clustering the work so it doesn't feel like a three-month campaign, actually all the work can be done in 6-10 hours and then you can focus on releasing it slowly.

Another question that comes up (this is people's fear), *what if I don't pre-sell any books?* Just trust that people are watching what you're doing. Sometimes they may not be responding to you or liking your posts and taking action and buying your books, but just be patient. Sometimes you will sell more books once your book launches because people see it and it's real.

But trust me, people are watching! Often people just like to observe and not get involved and once it comes out and they have that solid tangible proof, they will be taking action. So believe in yourself, believe in the value of the content that you have brought out and the message that you have got to share and before long you will see results. Trust me, you will build an amazing business growth from your book!

Chapter 9

Social Media Made Easy

It's no secret that today's world has turned into us being connected through the Internet. Our social life has become quite virtual and we often find people, even in restaurants or places where they hang out, looking at their smart phones and laptops. A lot of business growth and expansion of your business internationally will come from utilising platforms such as Facebook, LinkedIn, YouTube, Pinterest and many more social media platforms that have been utilised to this day.

It really is one of the fastest ways to grow your business online. In the next chapter I'll be covering a lot of offline methods of growing a business. In this chapter, I want to focus on specifically how to devise a social media strategy and how to grow your business exponentially, nationally, and internationally, through the use of social media.

The beauty of social media is that it's free! Well, most of it is free, of course you can pay for advertising on all your social media platforms, however, most of it can be done free if you do it the right way and you build those relationships over a long period of time.

Social media is fast, it's instant and actually it's a whole lot of fun! Not every person is suited to using these platforms but once you get going (you may feel awkward in the beginning, just trust and repeat the process) you will learn to love it.

It's a non-threatening way to do business and this is why gaining business through social media, for myself, doesn't feel like I'm selling! It does take time though; so always remember in any relationship building, whether it's online or offline, it takes time for people to get to know you, to like you, to interact with you and have a chat to you before they will buy from you.

I've been on social media since 2008 and I didn't see the business benefits from it for at least 18 months. Nowadays with a correct social media strategy this can happen a lot faster. I want to give you the fast track ways through which I've been able to help my own clients gain results a lot faster.

You get to really be able to connect with influential people that you normally wouldn't get to meet face to face. One of my favourite mentors in the world is Terry Hawkins; she wrote a book, *There Are Two Times In Life: Now and Too Late*. She's a gorgeous lady originally from Brisbane in Australia and now has expanded globally and has a business based in LA in the US. I met Terry Hawkins about 10 years ago at a conference I was attending for OPSM (back then I was in the optical industry). She spoke at one of our conferences and I was really inspired by her.

On that day I bought her book. I have followed and continue to be inspired by her. About two years ago I connected with her on Facebook. I sent her a message about what had happened (I sent a photo) to my copy of her book, which was all chewed up, because I had loaned it to a lot of people. I had read it myself four or five times. This started a conversation.

One day I saw that she was coming to Melbourne and I was super excited. I couldn't afford to attend her three-day training – I just didn't have the cash flow back then. I sent her a Facebook message saying that it's awesome that she's coming to my hometown to do training and that I would love to help out by being a crew member if she needed one. When you crew at events you generally attend them for free as you're helping out in the background.

I didn't hear from her for about 2-3 weeks and then I got this message three days before the event saying, "Oh my god Natasa, I'm so sorry I didn't get back to you, of course I'd love for you to come and crew!" She didn't mean that I needed to help out; she wanted me to be a participant at this particular training. Now this cost was in the thousands. I was beside myself. I rang up all my clients to reschedule and told them about the exciting news. I spent three amazing days with a mentor that has been one of the most influential people in my life, and someone that I've admired as a role model.

This is how social media assisted me to connect with someone who I believe is very influential as well as someone that I admire. I learned so much in those three days. We've continued to be connected in a closer way, going forward.

So remember, it's not just about getting business, but about the amazing relationships and connections that you can achieve through touching people through social media. Because it's a wonderful platform that is non-threatening and an easy way to do business without feeling that you're being a salesperson.

Another thing that social media is amazing for is for keeping your market up to date on your business and really adding high value content to them and building that trust over a period of time.

It's an essential ingredient in your marketing strategy for your book as well as for your ongoing business activities. Nowadays, I get up an hour before I need to have a meeting with anyone or chat to anyone and I spend one hour on my social media strategies.

At the back of the book in the Appendices, is a little spreadsheet that I do myself. Now this changes sometimes for the times where I actually post, however, that is what I use if I ever weren't consistent on social media. I will print off this little spreadsheet and actually tick myself off that I've posted in all the areas of the different pages that I posted. As you get more popular, perhaps you develop more than one brand, more than one fan page, you have lots of events coming up, you need to be posting regularly within these spots, so people are always reminded of what you're doing, they're following your stuff and you're really positioning yourself as that expert and go-to person.

In this particular chapter I really want to focus on just three specific social media platforms that I use, very consistently. I'm heavily involved in them because I'm a true believer that you cannot be great at 10-15 different platforms! So I focus on one and then I do a couple of other things that intertwine the three.

My top three are Facebook, LinkedIn and YouTube.

Facebook is my main platform and that is what I highly recommend. My target market is on Facebook so I make that my platform. If you're in a career where most of your target market hangs out on LinkedIn then you would choose that platform over Facebook. And realistically, YouTube is a channel that you develop, but you further share it through Facebook and LinkedIn. They then interconnect with each other.

Let's talk about some strategies!

Facebook

What I have found Facebook to be fantastic for is for building great national connections. So we are in Melbourne, Australia and I've been able to connect people all over the country. Why is this? Most of us are in a similar time zone and we are on social media around the same times. Most of the time people will use social media first thing in the morning, so that's 7-9am time-slot. So that's the best time to get on social media and post. And then you've got that evening time slot, again, 7-9 in the evenings would be the other time that people jump on and use social media. So you want to be on there half an hour in the morning, half an hour in the evening, or just do all your posts in the morning. Then you comment on a post and it bumps it back up into the news feeds. That means you cover the same information for morning and evening. So it's called "bumping" a post and you do that by commenting on your own post. Anything obviously, but you're not going to comment "bump" as I've seen people do!

It's very important that we continue to grow our connections on social media and one of the ways to do that is when you're offline marketing and networking and meeting people around the place, that you follow up with them and connect on social media to say how lovely it was to meet them. It's okay to also connect with people if you've heard of them and if you have mutual connections and then to start that conversation with them. You're building your network within the social media platforms.

When you build your network and you connect with people, there's no point in just adding a friend or just asking someone to be connected with you. It's very important to follow up, start and keep a conversation going. If someone connects with you, send them a private message and say it was awesome to connect. Say that you're curious about what prompted them to connect. Tell me a bit about yourself. Get people talking about themselves! When they do this the natural law of reciprocity says that they will ask you questions about yourself.

I find that it's really helpful to have templates already typed up ready to cut and paste from. Sometimes you need to be personal with people, so you type up a personal message. But when it's the initial introduction conversation, you can actually have a template typed up that says something quite short, casual. Be very, very casual when it comes to social media, after all we're meant to be social, not super professional!

Then you might want to have a secondary template that says a little bit more about what you do and has your contact details or your websites built into it because there's nothing more annoying than having to type up the same thing over and over. It's very ineffective and your productivity will be diminished. As you become more popular, or the well-known go-to person, you'll get a lot more connections coming your way and less need to connect with others.

Now you have to be very careful about who you connect with if you are going to connect with people that you don't personally know. If they say they don't know you, Facebook can actually freeze your account so you cannot friend any other people for 30 days. There are rules that apply, so you want to be careful. After all you want to be building relationships with people you've already met or someone you've heard of.

Use this particular platform to promote your events that are coming up. Make sure when you have your events listed that you continuously go into the news feed of that event to remind people that this is coming up and if they haven't signed up, this is their reminder. Very, very important, as the event gets close to 5 or 10 days that you're posting there daily. If it's further out then post every 2-3 days.

People ask me how regularly I should post on social media and I've heard some people go in there a couple of times a week. That's not enough for today's society! This is fast, instant. People want to be responded to so my recommendation would be 5-7 days per week.

Of course we need to have a day off, making sure that we add value and 5-7 days a week, but obviously on all your different pages, your personal page, your event page, your group pages. You need to post in lots of different areas. There's something that I must say here! Please don't post the same post all over the place because if people are following you, they're going to want to know different things about you.

Otherwise on their news feed, they're going to have the same post come up ten different times. What I do is always think of different things to say on my different pages. That way it keeps it fresh and people are getting tons of value rather than the same message ten times over because I've just been posting.

Focus on adding value. Your social media strategy should consist of 90% value and only 10% of offers and pitching. In saying that, three types of posts generally get put up.

1. Content and value adding posts.
2. You must remember to humanise your content. Share something from your life, your family; people want to know that you're just like them. Make people feel that you are their friend.
3. You can put up your special offers or invitations to your events and things like that.

So those are some of the basics around Facebook.

Let's go onto the LinkedIn musts!

LinkedIn

This platform is fantastic for national and international connections. I find with LinkedIn, the responses are not as quick. People can get back to you in 2-3 days rather than the same day and this is why I find it works well for international connections, because those people may be in a different time zone, but when you get their message you could go back and forward with them.

LinkedIn Forums and groups are fantastic for getting people to review your profiles and they can connect with you and start that conversation and find out a bit more. It is very important that you have a fantastic profile written up. If you don't know how to write it yourself, ask someone who has a great one. Maybe they can help you out and you can actually pay to have a LinkedIn profile done professionally.

LinkedIn is like a resume online of all the things that you've done. People can actually leave recommendations, which is a very, very powerful tool. It builds up your social proof around your expertise. People can also endorse you in terms of the skills that you have that they believe you possess. When you build this up to a really high level, you start having an awesome presence and a strong profile and people often will in turn connect with you without you needing to connect with others.

One of my favourite questions and responses when people connect with me on LinkedIn is, "How did you find out about me?" the second question is, "What was it about my profile that prompted you to connect?" If people connect with us they may have read something on our profile that helps them and this actually gets the conversation going. You'd be amazed at the sort of response it gets from people and how they will further interact with you.

When it comes to your profile, do look over it every 3-6 months to ensure that it's up to date and continue to ask people to write recommendations within your profile, because those recommendations could truly be the sales tool that is going to get someone to want to connect to you and talk to you.

Often via LinkedIn, if someone is local in my area, I would ask them to catch up for coffee. And it's great to ask people nowadays to catch up for coffee even online, via Skype. So ask, "would you like to have a coffee personally or over Skype" and just work out how you guys can get to know each other and how you can help one another.

Always ask for people to catch up and have your follow up systems in place because it is very important to follow up. Again use your little templates to introduce yourself, to open up the casual conversations. In time, when you're too busy to look after this part of the business you can pass over these templates to a virtual assistant, someone who can manage this system for you so that you don't stop doing it altogether.

It's very important to be consistent on social media. You cannot disappear off social media and expect to have the same momentum when you return. So often when I travel, I am on social media and I'm letting people know what I'm doing. I'm posting pictures up of my holiday or whatever and this is the thing that is super-powerful around building my personal brand, because at the end of the day it depends on what you do. I help people write their books to build their business. I'm selling a lifestyle! So if people see me on holidays, enjoying myself, having my family time, having that great balance, that's what people will buy into – the emotional angle.

And that's the thing that you need to remember: what do your clients come to you for emotionally? How can you perhaps portray that through social media?

Now we come to my third most used platform.

YouTube

I won't spend too much time on this because I've already covered it but YouTube is just a fantastic way to link up and get people to see you. When you record your videos, upload them into YouTube and then share them on your LinkedIn, Twitter, or on your Facebook platforms, it's a great way to get people interacting with you and a great way to actually get them to subscribe to your channel.

Now something that recently did on my channel, is put some channel art onto it, so it makes it customised. I've put myself and my books up there. It really does grab someone's attention to have an introduction video and gets them to subscribe to it. Lastly, I have integrated and I've had someone through Fiverr.com help me, for $5, integrate the

YouTube link via an image tab on my Facebook fan page. If you visit any of my fan pages you can see that my YouTube channel is built into my Facebook fan pages.

It's absolutely amazing, the things that you can do and how you can link up your social media platforms.

So here are my top 5 social media musts.

1. Be consistent with your posts and practice patience in the early days.
2. Watch your behaviour and perception you're building.
3. Focus on building relationships; it's no different from face-to-face networking.
4. Add value to people; mix up personal posts, value posts and sale type posts.
5. Build your friends and connections consistently with everyone you meet when you're out and about and have your templates ready for a quick follow up.

There's so much more that we can share around social media, however this has been condensed within one chapter so that you guys can have the basics and that you can have a lot of fun with it and you can build an amazing business through the power of social media. I consistently do it and I can say that over 90% of my business comes from social media and from any other marketing strategies.

So I strongly encourage you to make this part of your everyday activities and set aside that time and treat it as your work time.

It truly is, yes it is fun! And on my weekends I treat it like fun. During the week, it is part of my daily business activities.

Go off and be social!

Chapter 10

Personal Marketing Channels

One of the strongest and most powerful ways to grow your business when you start out and when your book is released is through three different ways of connecting with people. Those include networking, workshops and running your own webinars. Two of them are offline and one is online and I believe that they link quite nicely together and it's very important to talk about all of these as one. It's really about building that relationship in a face-to-face way and adding value to people through what you do and sharing your message by building a community and a tribe of followers around you.

Let's touch on them separately and work out what the benefits for each one are. When we're talking about workshops I will be giving you distinctions between a workshop and a webinar, because most of the information is exactly the same when it comes to talking about workshops versus webinars, except webinars are online seminars for workshops, so many of the ideas are exactly the same for those two. Networking is slightly different.

Networking

Networking is one of the fastest ways to grow your business in the start up stage. Now we've become a business owner we need to grow our network, because there's a famous saying, *your network equals your net worth!* This was the number one way that I grew my business in the early days.

I focused a lot of networking and building those relationships and discovering opportunities to connect with people that would assist me in getting the business that I was after. You get to be surrounded by people that are ahead of you or are at the same level as you, therefore you're interacting with like-minded people as well as successful people that you can explore and learn different ideas from.

So many times I have received a lot of free advice, or low-cost advice from my networking connections. It truly is an investment in the long term when it comes to building a relationship, because we all know, to build that trust, likeability, and connection with people, it takes a long time.

With networking you're looking at about six to eight times of people seeing you and getting to know you before they would look at helping you. Really put that goal out there and make sure that you make networking a strategy and don't expect too much to happen in the first 6-8 months.

You get to surround yourself with people that are getting the results you want, which means that there's another famous saying that *your net worth is the average of the five people that you hang around with*.

So really think about that and as you grow in your business – and personally – do expand and change the groups that you go to if you feel that you have outgrown them.

This has happened to me and my business. I've heard a successful entrepreneur out there also say that *if you are the smartest person in the room, then you're in the wrong room!* So you need to go to places where people are going to stretch you, challenge you and be able to educate you on things that you perhaps don't know quite yet.

I think networking builds a wonderful platform to start new friendships as well. It's a whole lot of fun, people give people energy. That personal connection that we lack so much nowadays, because we've gone so online and virtual, is when it has its power and it really does aid in you increasing your confidence in public speaking skills.

It really is something that you will benefit from if not so much in monetary ways, but in personal ways that will make you a more successful business in turn.

Networking is about sharing information, ideas, resources and opportunities. Members of a network look to each other for advice, tips on jobs, careers and business opportunities. It is about developing trust amongst yourself and the people that you network with.

It is a long-term business commitment that will benefit your businesses in time.

There are many different types of networking groups and we won't go into too much detail because we're really just taking a helicopter view over some of these concepts around networking workshops and seminars. What I encourage you to do as a result of learning these strategies is to look up some literature around specific books on networking. Specific books that talk about running your own workshops and then running your own webinars, because there is a lot of information out there that goes into a whole lot more detail than we could in this particular book.

These are all ways that you can further sell your book and then leverage your business through these three forms of marketing. So with networking as I've suggested before, laminate your book cover and go around and show people that this is coming up. When they're interested in your book, it opens up the corridor for a lot more conversations around what you do, how you do it and potentially gaining clients from that.

In generic terms, the type of networking groups that are out there depends where you are and what's available, but there's many groups that meet where they have a rigid structure. Some are very timed, there's certain rules, there's certain ways you find referrals for one another and the commitment can vary with networking groups from a weekly commitment to a monthly commitment in most cases.

There are groups that are specifically designed for women. Networking groups where there are women only, because it's been shown that women network a specific way. If your business is more relevant to a woman, then you might consider these types of events to attend. If you're a male business owner and your business target's women that might be a little difficult, but there is the option there for women-only networking events. They're also a bit gentler, because new business owners can feel very self-conscious, and fear putting themselves out there to pitch their ideas.

There's networking events, which are council organised. There are meet-up groups where people organise their events online and then meet up together and then there's the opportunity for you, yourself, as a business owner, to run your own networking event.

I've been running my own networking event for the last year and it's an amazing way to position yourself as a leader. Not only are you positioning yourself through your book as a credible expert and a go-to person, you will also position yourself and be seen as that leader if you set up your own networking group.

Now I don't suggest doing this too early in your business. What you want to make sure you have is an established network. You have been out networking, you've met lots of people, you've connected with them, you've got your contact details, so when you launch your own networking event you have people to invite and from there you can grow it over a period of time.

Initially, you may have a small group of people and as more people find out about it, you will grow your networking group to get ideas on how to structure your event. The experience of attending other people's events and other people's structured formats will give you an idea of how you can put yours together.

So think about what events might suit your business and I highly encourage you to start visiting some.

Now something I really want to address here is what networking is NOT.

- Turning up and selling yourself to people who you meet; treating everyone as a prospect
- Giving out your business card and expecting to do business
- About meeting everyone in the room for a brief moment
- Looking at in the way of 'what's in it for me?'
- Talking about yourself first
- You looking interested versus interesting (** ted versus ting).

Remember all those things that you shouldn't do. I look at it as though I'm going to places to meet other business owners and to make some new friends, rather than going to sell my business and look for opportunities and clients.

My top three master networker's tips for you would be:

1. Have an elevator speech, no longer than 60 seconds. If you would like to get a template for this type of speech, I'm more than happy for you to email me and I will send you a template.
2. Use your personality to engage others so they remember you. Build rapport. Remember, no one likes to be around grumpy people. So

do remember to build rapport with people when you meet them and really manage your state when you're around other people.

3. Look successful, have your business cards ready and shake hands firmly.

If you want to build a strong network strategy, I have developed 5 steps you must follow:

1. Find and register to events. Make sure you attend two events regularly.
2. Turn up even when you don't feel like it, because most events are early in the mornings, however there are some evening ones.
3. Book in two coffee chats from each event; catch up with people outside of the event one-on-one. This is where the true networking relationship happens.
4. Follow up, follow up, follow up! That is within 24-48 hours; connect with people on social media as well as via a nice follow up email. You might even like to do a template around this.
5. Always look at how you can help your networking buddies, because if you have the philosophy that givers gain, then by giving to others and helping others out, you in turn will be taken care of.

Let's now move onto the workshop and webinars marketing strategies. Again I'm going to mention that I'll do these side by side, because many of the principles I will teach you apply to both.

Running workshops and webinars is an amazing marketing tool for your business, especially when you're new and no one knows who you are and what you do, because when people can see, touch and feel you and this is talking about the workshops, then they can really go and see the value and grow to trust and like you.

Workshops and webinars are about instant product creation and a definite way of gaining feedback as to where you're at and what you need to improve for next time. You get to share your passion. You get to then have a platform to up-sell to a bigger program, package or products. What an amazing way to boost your confidence and certainty in terms of what you have to offer.

I can remember the first time I ran my first workshop. It was a 45-minute workshop and it took me 20 days leading up to it, to practice my talk because I was just so nervous. That's the thing with running workshops and webinars for the first time, you will feel awkward. It's not going to be comfortable. You will probably shake and you will quiver in your voice and sweaty palms and all of the above. With time I promise you will learn to love them and have that excited butterfly type of feeling – excited energy rather than nervous energy.

My first webinar! I had it scripted from the first thing I said to the last thing I said. I was so nervous that I wouldn't be able to think on my feet, that I would say a lot of erms and errs and that I wouldn't come across well.

Nowadays I just turn up and I just start talking. I'm very natural and that just comes with practice.

The most important thing about workshops or webinars is about having the fun engaging the audience. It is about their energy and working out that sensory acuity to know what they need. It's about making it an inclusive environment so if you're in a webinar it's not just talking at people. Stop every five minutes, asking for feedback, comments, questions and queries and really serving the room or the webinar as to what it needs.

It is very important that for both of these you are organised, professional, on time, you're running things as smoothly and effortlessly as possible. No one should know the organisation that is probably happening in the background. It's a fantastic way to give people more values. It's great to give away some gifts and bonuses when you're running workshops and webinars. That's what makes an amazing webinar or workshop.

And definitely, the last thing that makes them amazing is that you have an irresistible offer where people can take that next step. And if you have wet their appetite through this particular workshop and webinar, they should take that next step, because if you don't offer it to them they will go looking for it somewhere else.

Here I want to give you the five secrets to running your own workshops and webinars.

1. Start with your date! Consider this before you choose the date. If it's a workshop, I would be giving 4-6 weeks lead-in time. If it's a webinar about 7-10 days. Because webinars are a lot more instant and people generally won't sit around waiting for them to come around in six weeks' time.
2. Have a sexy name! So remember your title of your workshop and webinar needs to sell people what they want and give them what they need. If you don't know what I'm talking about go back to the earlier chapters and look up what I mean by sexy names.
3. Get bums and seats or people on the call. The marketing! There are many different ways that you can market and those are online and offline. If you're learning your business you'll find that your offline strategy through networking to be the most powerful way to fill your workshops and webinars. As you grow your database your email marketing and your social media events, you can post there for people to see. You could pay for some Google Adwords or pay some further advertising to promote your event. There are many different formats and it's one of the most challenging areas in people's businesses. This is where you have your sexy outline; you need to tell them all the benefits and sell them what they want. Make sure that

your marketing plan and intention behind filling the room is a very action-focused and that there's regular communication and reminders. You need to tell people lots of times that your event is coming up, because the majority of people may not notice it. Sometimes people need to see something 3-5 times to take action on it. A site that I use for my events is EventBright.com.au. You can set up your event and then you can send people a link so that they'll pay and register for it. It's amazing and it doesn't cost a thing. Your people registering pay the fees in terms of the small percentage that the website keeps. It's the way they make their money, however it's a wonderful platform and you can share your events via social media.

4. Get organised! Structure your workshops and webinars. Use the format system of the *why, what, how and what if*. I explained this earlier in this book. This is the same way you can structure your PowerPoint presentations when you're running a workshop or a webinar. People don't need to know that there is chaos behind the scenes, because when you arrive at your workshop or webinar, everything should be running as it should. It's very important to have the proper preparation, the proper checklists; everything set up in the room correctly, that you've arrived early, that you have centred yourself, that you have done a little bit of a visualisation if that's what you need to do and take in a few deep breaths and as soon as people start to turn up. You are on and you're marketing yourself from the moment they walk into that room to the moment they walk out. Always remember that you must be organised. I've included a checklist in the Appendices for what to take if you're running workshops. It should be helpful.

5. Test and measure everything that you do. Ensure that you collect feedback, especially if it's in workshops. Usually on webinars you wouldn't collect feedback, but you might ask people via an email afterwards how they found it. You want to test and measure your

sales. Did you get and were you happy with your conversion in terms of who took your irresistible offer? Was your offer popular and what did people think about it? So test and measure; test and measure. It's super important so that you can adjust and change whatever needs to be changed in the future so that you get better outcomes and you just keep improving.

The last thing I'm going to say around workshops and webinars is that it's very important to follow up. Follow up is crucial! I suggest sending out two or three follow up emails or a little postcard. What I used to do is take a photo of the whole group that was at the live workshop and put it into a system that I use for sending out postcards and I would post everyone out a photo of that particular moment. It's very important to follow up, you might like to give people an additional bonus in the follow up stages and providing recordings of the actual webinar. This is very valuable, because people who missed it can listen to the recording and then get back to you. You can pick up additional sales this way, from those workshops and webinars that perhaps didn't happen in the room.

Networking, workshops, and webinars are such big marketing tools for businesses and any business can do them. Not just coaches or consultants or trainers or facilitators, but any business could educate other people and add value to other people through a workshop or a webinar and gain more exposure and grow their list through running and going along to events and presenting themselves as a leader.

Go and do them. You will sell lots of books from the back end of your workshops and webinars as well as networking and it's a way that your local community will know who you are as well as through your webinars. You will gain an international following as long as you do them consistently and you keep improving and adjusting and looking for the feedback. You can grow and learn and expand and get to new and high levels within your business.

Chapter 11

Weekend Aftermath

You've done it You've completed your book in 48 hours! How amazing is that? When you started reading this book, you didn't think it was possible. Well it certainly is and you have proven that you have been able to do it. And if you haven't done it, then go back and do the actions I have asked you to do in the previous chapters so that you can move forward in terms of handing your book over to the professionals to do all the cleaning up and typing up for you.

The different things that you need to consider about the handover of your book post the weekend, come in line with what you need to do around your website in terms of getting your pre-sales set up. How to hand over your transcriptions over to the transcriptionist of your choice and how to hand over your book in the form of a manuscript to your publisher who will publish your book.

Those are the things I want to give you some information about because if you don't have everything created in the correct order, or you're missing bits and pieces, then it's important that you go back and get this stuff together before you hand it across so that the process is smooth and effortless and you can get your book published as soon as possible.

When you're handing over the information to the person who will do your website ensure that you actually have everything you need to give them in one email. If you've created a promotional video for your book website, you need to put your link inside that email. You want to attach the photo of yourself, the headshot and the little 3D widget of your book.

You need to insert your 'About the Author' section. You need your little sexy blurb that is going to make people hungry to buy your book. Everything that you need to hand over to the person who is doing your website should go across in one neat email so they can pull all that information out and set it up for you promptly and without anything missing. I can't tell you how many times we've had people work with website developers and oftentimes they're sending their information sporadically or one at a time and it just ends up being a lengthier process than it should be rather than getting everything sent across at once. Don't send everything until you can put it all together. So if you've done a video, or you want to do the video first, then send it across with the other bits and pieces.

It's also important that you're well organised when you're handing your recordings to your transcriptionist. When you've been recording your chapters you should clearly mark what chapter it is. When I start this chapter I always say the chapter name and title. It doesn't mean it can't change later on as it most likely will. As I'm recording this I'm speaking it out. Make sure that everything is clearly named so that your transcriptionist gets them back to you in that particular order. This makes the cutting and pasting process when you create a big manuscript for your publisher a lot easier. Ensure that you create a Dropbox folder, which you can share with him or her and ensure that you communicate with them effectively. Estimate that it's going to take someone approximately two weeks to complete the transcription of your work.

For hiring a transcriptionist I suggest trying someone via Elance.com or Odesk.com, which is where people will bid for your business to do the transcription work for you. Ensure that you also do a little bit of research on the person in terms of what their background is. Is English their first language if your book is written in English? That doesn't mean people won't be reading this book in other languages, however ensure that their native language is the language that you're also writing in, so that you can get high quality work and you will find transcriptionists out there who have had experience in transcribing books and chapters for people so they actually end up structuring it a little bit neater and nicer for you and develop a good end product for you.

Do your homework. You can even ask to test someone out. Send them a 5-10 minute recording and they can do a page or two for you just to show you how it's coming across and usually a lot of people will be happy to do this because the whole project or book would be a good amount of income for them to get from you.

Get your files across and ensure that you ask your transcriptionist if possible to send them back to you as he or she is going along the process, so then at your end you can start cleaning them up, ensuring that everything is set up the way you like it.

Once you receive your files back from your transcriptionist, it is important that you read through them and you do one final clean up and reshuffle things, cut and paste them where you want them to appear. Sometimes if you have recorded different sections, you may not have named them as per chapter. You may want to now select where they're going to go. Is there going to be little sub-titles in your sections? Are there any bullet points you want to add in? What kind of diagrams and illustrations do you want to appear and where?

Read through it or get someone else to read through it. Don't be too picky, because your editor and publisher will go through and clean up things like grammatical, spelling errors and things like that. You just want to make sure that it sounds the way you want your book to come across.

What we're aiming for now is we're going to speak about the handover of your book manuscript. What we're really aiming for here is that your book ends up being somewhere between 40-45,000 words to hand over to your publisher. This is a decent sized book, which when formatted will end up giving you about 150-160 pages. If you have illustrations and diagrams or appendices, then you may have a few more pages than that, that's okay. Decent-sized books are about that size and this is something to aim for. On the 48 Hour Weekend, we suggest to our authors to aim for that many words.

You want to submit all your documents that you've gotten back from the transcriptionist. Put everything into one file, this is now called a manuscript. And also put them in the order that they should appear in. Clean it up as much as possible to make sure that the editor can understand everything.

Now to work out what order they should appear in. You can look at other books and then you can actually submit the order that you want things to appear in, because you've seen it in a book and you want to model it. Here is one order that I recommend from experience.

One thing to not worry about yourself is the contents page in your book. This is something your publisher will add into the formatting stages, because you don't know where it's going to end up, what section, what page, so they do that at the very end for you.

So the order you want to see and submit your document in, this is a suggested order, not set in concrete.

1. Testimonials
2. Dedication

3. Introduction
4. Chapters
5. Afterward
6. About the Author
7. Any special offers and calls to action at the back of the book; sponsorships that you may have got off people to take part in your book that you can pop in there, that would be also an opportunity for you to put that at the back of the book.

Sometimes your publisher will come back to you and say you have a few spare pages because each print run is a certain amount of pages.

When you're submitting your illustrations, any diagrams or pictures, do submit them separately, but attach them in the same email or file, perhaps you're going to share a Dropbox folder with your publisher, where you will have your pictures separate.

Then the editing and the formatting process, the cleaning up happens. Usually, it will depend on the company that you deal with. With a publisher, it all happens generally within a month. Sometimes they take up to three months of back and forward communication. It's usual when working with a publisher to go back and forward about three or four times for any adjustments and to check that the start and the finish of my book has all the correct details. Really check out the layout and what it looks like.

I personally don't read over it again, you can if you're a more detailed person, but what I'm trying to say here is do let go of it, because the quicker you get your book out there, the faster you can start leveraging your business via your book. And it truly isn't about being perfect. It's about getting your message out there and having some fun with it and growing your business.

So let it go. One of my favourite sayings is *it's perfect the way it is!* That's how it is when I do things. Armed with all this information in hand, it really is keeping it simple. Ensure that you are sending content through in one hit to people and another big tip that I have for you is to ensure that there's clear communication. If a person has told you that something will come through at a certain time and hasn't, do follow up. Sometimes we're not aware of what's happening in other people's lives and it could be something quite horrible. Like one time when I was getting the illustrations done for my very first book, *The 7 Ultimate Secrets to Weight Loss*, the person who was doing illustrations for me lost her mum. I wasn't aware of that, I did follow up and didn't get a response for a little while, then she told me what happened. So never assume that they're being lazy or not doing their job, but do follow up and be prompt with their follow ups.

Use positive language. Never assume, especially if it's people that you cannot see face to face. One of the best things that you can do in business is to build in buffers for yourself. That way, if something doesn't go according to plan, you're not working to a really set deadline that if you don't meet it, the world will fall apart.

Ensure that you're always getting things done ahead of your deadline so if unexpected circumstances occur, you have that buffer of time to make up what you need to make up. I can't emphasise this strongly enough, because otherwise you may get stuck in some very uncomfortable positions and you may not be able to follow through as to what you've promised in your business. So I always work well ahead of what my real deadlines are to make things happen. Under promise and over deliver rather than the other way around.

Another way to fast track your process to getting your book into your hands as soon as possible is to ensure that you are prompt in your replies to the people that are working with you. Your website person, your transcriptionist, your publisher. If they send you an email, make sure you action it within 24 hours and send a response back because the longer they wait on your response, the longer it will take for their adjustments to come back to you.

As soon as I'm working with other people, the minute they send something through to me, I always go for finding the nearest empty slot of time that I can to respond back to them so that I can get my work finalised as soon as possible. Always allow yourself a bit of extra time when it comes to graphic design work, because I find that graphic design work can take the longest out of anything that you can do with outsourcing to people, because graphic design work is something that is very personal. If the person that you're working with is not getting your vision down in the design you may need to go back and forward a lot of times. This is why the designers often give you unlimited revisions and that's something to really build in a super buffer for, especially if you're a picky person and you need slight changes and it takes you 10-20 times going back and forward with people.

So, good luck with all your outsourcing. This is a project that you can definitely manage yourself. We do it for our authors at the weekend to make it easier and that's part of the service. But you can definitely do it yourself and have an amazing outcome. Practice patience, be prompt in your replies and always speak in a positive language. Look towards coming up with a solution to whatever query you have and definitely give people a go and never assume anything until you know the full story and the reasons for any delays.

All the best!

Chapter 12

10 Easy Steps to Bust Your Money Limiting Beliefs

People nowadays love to get into business, but they find it so difficult to ask for the sale. Selling is something that a lot of us cringe at. I was one of those people and it was very tough for me to ask and tell people what I was worth per hour. I have worked a lot on myself over the past three and a half years and changed a lot of my beliefs when it comes to money. When we were away at our first Ultimate 48 Hour Author Weekend a lot of this talk came up in the informal sections of our weekend. I decided on the second day of the weekend, that I would create a bonus segment where I would tell people what the ten things are that I have done to overcome some of my money-limiting beliefs. I continue to do these on a daily basis to bust through my money blueprint.

We are born with a money blueprint and unless we know how to break through this and change our beliefs about money, we tend to end up earning the same amount of money, no more, no less, most of our lives! This comes from that imprint period between one and seven where, as children, we hear things from our parents, like "money doesn't grow on trees", "money is the root of all evil". There is also a translated saying from Macedonia where I grew up and that is "money is a killer." So if you've been told these kinds of things when you were growing up you will have built beliefs about money being dirty, evil, no good, too hard to come by.

How are we possibly meant to build great beliefs about receiving money and making a difference in the world through our passion and being paid for it? Through this repetition over the years, those beliefs keep being embedded into our subconscious. Even though we might consciously say, “no, I don’t think money is dirty or I don’t think it’s the root of all evil”, somewhere in the subconscious level it still resides and it takes some work to see a change in your money blueprint and financial abundance in your life.

I always say to people that to change a neural pathway it takes 2-3 years or 1000 times of repetition to build that neural pathway. I believe that sometimes it’s an ongoing journey on working on yourself and building strong, new beliefs to create some new neural pathways about what you think is possible. What I would say is there are rich people that are not nice people, but there are also rich people that are wonderful people. I believe there’s a balance in the world.

There are 50% of people who have good intentions and 50% perhaps have not so good intentions. That principle still applies whether you are rich or poor. The universe tends to provide this balance and I often love reading the work of Doctor John D Martini, who talks about this, that there is always this equilibrium and that’s what you also have to remember within your own life and around your beliefs and strengths and weaknesses that you probably have a half of each.

I want to give you some practical tools that I have used over the last three and a half years that have definitely shifted my money blueprint. I can now assist so many more people and touch so many more business owners worldwide through my book creations, my licenses, the people that I help one on one. It’s just been an amazing journey and I’m only able to do that because I feel blessed to be rewarded financially and I believe that there is that fair exchange. We’re going to talk about that a little bit later on.

For now let's go through all the different steps that you can take to bust through your money-limiting beliefs. You can have a more abundant future financially if you build a mindset around that. Especially if you're wanting to leverage your business through your book, because the only way you're going to create that 6-7 figure income is by being able to ask for the sale. You need to feel fantastic about receiving money for what you provide to people.

1. Build your own money affirmations. For all our lives we have been affirmed all negative things about money. "Money is the root of all evil" or "money doesn't grow on trees", during our early childhood years. It is now time to reprogram that! And something that you will need to be reading every single day. So not all of my affirmations have to do with money, however, I do have 2-3 that serve me fantastically when it comes to money. I say, "money is my friend", "money flows easily to me." Those are some of the things that I repeat to myself every single day. They're very powerful and what I also know is that if I don't love money, why would money love me back? Just think of it in a way if you are with your partner and you constantly were acting as if you don't want them in your life, what would they do? They would leave! So that's the same thing as money. If you're always acting as if money is not important, you don't love it, all that kind of stuff, then money is going to leave you in no time and it's going to be the easy come, easy go, or it won't come at all. So affirmations are my first practical tool for you to implement in your life and there's so many you can think of. You can even look them up on Google if you can't think of any for yourself.

2. Insure that you have a nice, expensive, wallet that you carry cash in. We have become a plastic society and every time I see people (and this is 99% of people), they deal with cards. Why is this? Well it used to be my belief, and I was exactly this person, that if I had cash in my wallet I would spend it. And I did so I had proved my-

self right. When I attended a Neurolinguistic programming training, the trainer suggested that, in order to have the abundance mindset (where we feel secure and safe and abundant financially) we should invest in a very expensive wallet. Make sure that we clean it out weekly, that it doesn't have any receipts or loose, messy bits of paper and carry cash in it. Not small amounts of cash, like $20 or $50. Carry around as much cash as you want to earn every single day. And so I did that, I started doing that earlier this year and I never spend the money! Sometimes I might dip into $50 if I'm starved, but I carry around a lot of cash in my wallet, everywhere I go. Guess what? I feel really great, because if I had to pay for something or I need it quickly I know I've got it there. That makes me feel great. Every time I open up my wallet I see lots of $50 notes and it makes me feel really safe, even though that may be a contradiction to some of you reading this. It's like, "Oh my god what if you get robbed with a few thousand dollars in your wallet?" I just don't think of that! I don't want to focus on a scarcity mentality; I focus on an abundance mentality. I have a Chanel wallet that my mum actually purchased for me seven years ago and it looks brand new still, so if you invest in something expensive, value it and do use it! You don't have to have 15 different wallets. It's good enough if you have one nice one and value it. This is a very important tip in terms of building that abundance mentality.

3. Split your money up in terms of how you choose to use it. What we do in our family is we live off 60%, we put aside 30% for tax and we put aside 10% in our "Pay Ourselves First" account. Now a lot of you may have read books where it's been said that 10% should always go into pay yourself first off everything that you earn and furthermore, in future, that this is money you're going to invest in passive income-generating assets that will provide financial independence in your later years. When we started doing this about 6-7 months ago, what I have found has shifted is that I

have attracted even more money in my life. I'm still able to live off that 60%, I don't need to spend every single dollar that's coming through. When the tax bill comes, I'm relaxed! I've got the money. I just hand it over and it's dealt with. That money doesn't even count. And then I also look at my investment account growing really consistently. As we're in a business and the income can shift and often shifts in an upward direction every three months I have a look at my reconciliations and work out how much we have increased, so that I can reset my amounts that I put aside every single week. What we do is that we have direct debits set up for that 30% and 10% that go into two other accounts and we don't even see or feel it. When it's set up on automatic pilot, like direct debits, then it makes it a lot easier to do it. You're not even going into the computer and generating that transfer every single week. So for mindset purpose, it's so much easier to just have whatever amount come out for 30% and whatever amount that is 10% and just focus on making do with the 60% that's coming through. It's possible and I can tell you that you will only be given more by the universe, because if the universe can see that you can manage your money right, it's okay to give you more. The last thing it would want for you is to get stuck. Say you've generated a million dollars of sales and you have to pay out $300,000 in tax, if you have not put anything aside your business could go bust overnight and you could be out on the street! People who know how to manage their money correctly and plan for the different areas that they've got to take care of, are those people that will be given a lot more and will attract more abundance in their lives.

4. The feedback loop. When I started out, I was charging $125 per hour. Now that's heading towards well over $500 an hour. How did I actually come to a point to increase my prices, so to $500 versus what I was charging 3 years ago? Well I have grown! I have seen the results. I'm able to give people and assist people and I

get the feedback. They report back to me how quickly they have seen the changes in their businesses and their lives. Therefore, I know that I am valuable and I feel that it is time to increase the price. What took me 12 months to work with a client a year ago, let's say, versus today, takes me 1-2 months of work. Really, the price point then is relative to how fast you can get them the results. So if you're ever wondering when is it time to increase your prices, I would say the time is when you know you have grown, you are able to help people faster, more efficiently. You're to a point and where your value increases, because you can do the same amount of work in two hours that used to take you 10 hours to do at a lower price point.

5. This is your language. You really need to change the language around how you view the things that you want to purchase in your life. So oftentimes we automatically ask ourselves, "can I afford this?" or "Do I have money to buy that?" Change it and insert the word "how" in front of those two questions. How can I afford this? How can I find the money to be able to have this in my life? So putting in the word "how", all of a sudden puts your mind into action to work out what steps you need to take it into reality for yourself. It really works and it's an open-ended question. Rather than "can I afford this" yes or no, and then you stop thinking. Rather, then, "how can I afford this" all of a sudden opens up a variety of choices, of what are the actions you can take? Do you need to work harder? Do you need to find another client? Do you need to find another five clients depending on what it is you want to purchase or be able to afford and buy for yourself? So change your language around money and change how you see the purchases that you want to make.

6. Set some specific goals. I've been a goal-setter since my late teens and I even do it much more specifically nowadays in the

format that I have developed and what I have found is that oftentimes when people start to goal-set, they set their goals way too high and they're unrealistic about them and they're not specific enough in terms of what actions they need to take to make that a reality. I did this myself as well. When I started out I remember proclaiming that in my first six months of business I would make $100,000. Well little did I know what it takes to actually get to a six-figure income and it actually took me two and a half years to get to that six-figure income and from there it's just grown exponentially. There's been a lot of foundation building, a lot of product creation, a lot of writing and a lot of relationship building in those years, leading up to the point where I am today. However, when I realised I was being really unrealistic with my goals, I put them right back and started off small. First of all my goal was to get to $500 per week in my business. Once I reached that, to $750 a week to $1000 a week. I kept just inching it up, and setting myself really specific and measurable goals and backing them up with the actions I need to take to make them a reality. If you want to know more about goal-setting and the Natasa Denman way of setting goals, email me and I can send you my ebook on goal-setting. It's about a 20 page ebook which I'm happy to share with you because I think it's very important and my system has worked really well for a lot of people, so I'd love to share it with you.

7. Stop being wasteful! I see way too many business-owners out there invest in a lot of education, a lot of quick fixes. They suffer from the shiny object syndrome and they end up not implementing everything that they actually invest in. I'm not saying you have to implement absolutely everything, but I would expect at least 80% of what you invest in, that you implement into your business after all. If you haven't, then you've wasted a lot of money and hard-earned cash. Plan for where your money is going to go. Think three times about investing in that program. Oftentimes I suggest,

walk away from a presentation or a seminar and think about what was happening at that seminar. Think about whether you really need the product or the service that you're being sold. I know a lot of people early on in business can get caught up in the hype and really get attracted to the magic bullet solutions that are being provided out there. And at the end of the day, these people after all need to market their program, just like you're marketing your book, your programs and everything in them in a sexy way, selling that magic bullet. However, do gain that self-awareness of where perhaps you might be doing things in the heat of the moment. Step aside from it. The deal will be still available if it's the right thing for you after that presentation.

8. Ensure that you know and are aware of what your budget is. Ensure that you know what your core is. Are you living within your means or are you living outside of your means? Ensure that you do your budget and what it takes to cover all your expenses every 3-6 months. Because as your business grows and shifts, so will your expenses and it's important that you keep a finger on this. Often people just give money and they don't realise that they're actually living outside their means and they're stacking up tons of credit, which is something that drains a lot of money through interest rates. So awareness around your budget is key! This is again being smart and managing your money, like an adult, and not spending every time you see the next shiny object. There are many websites that you can visit where you can download budget templates. There are many people that are great with their money and that you can ask for them to help you come up with a budget. I strongly recommend that you find out exactly where you're at, even if it's not something you want to see. The only way out of that situation is to actually face it and then change your actions and your strategy going forward.

9. Fair exchange and keeping the balance. When we provide a service or a product to someone and vice versa when we receive a service or product from someone, energy exchanges hands. And the energy that exchanges hands in one direction, which could be the product and service in the other direction, must be the money. So if you've been uncomfortable about asking for the sale and receiving money for the products or services that you provide through your business, then think again. Number one: people would not value what you do if they don't pay for it. People will not make the changes you want them to make if they don't pay for it, because at the end of the day you need to have skin in the game. Sometimes, there needs to be that financial pain that you have invested in, that's going to make you take the action. I've had a mentor since month three into my business and for over three and a half years now I have invested in a mentor monthly. Now my mentor tells me everything I've done, because I don't want to be wasteful, if I'm investing in something I'm not going to waste it. So fair exchange is asking the fair price that you're worth. I could never ask $500 per hour back at day one, because that wouldn't have been a fair exchange. I wasn't able to deliver $500 of value in one hour! Nowadays I'm congruent and I believe with my whole heart and soul that I'm worth that $500 an hour when I speak to people and they actually tell me that it's well worth more than that! I feel comfortable charging that, and yes, my intention is always to deliver higher value than the asking price. That should always be your intention as well. If you undercharge yourself, you may feel resentful in terms of what you get back, the energy back from the people that work with you. Vice versa if you overcharge, other people will feel ripped off and feel like they didn't get what they paid for. So think about fair exchange and think about energy exchange rather than money exchange. Because money is just a form of energy that we exchange for the value that we provide for our products and services.

10. Ensure that you reward yourself and celebrate! When you achieve those goals, go and buy yourself something if there's something you want. I always used to have a little reward after gaining a new client, or a big reward, when I reached my 20 clients, or a certain figure in my business. I would celebrate and I would go and enjoy that reward and I would look forward to the next one. I'd have things on my vision board and as I achieve them I can replace them with something else. It really is something that you must do for yourself. You must show love for yourself and you must show acknowledgement and recognition for yourself.

Here I just want to add in one other bonus tip and that is practicing gratitude. For the last 200 days straight, I have a gratitude journal. And I have written down ten things every day that I have been grateful for that have happened in that day. And can you believe it? I have not had a bad day in the last 200 days. Because you know what? When you practice gratitude, you're focusing on what you already have, which most likely is way more than if you compared yourself to a lot of people in the rest of the world.

What you're failing to focus on is what's missing and that's what I believe the biggest change in my life, especially in the last six months, has been through practicing daily gratitude. I always sit down in the evening and I write down the ten things that I was grateful for in the day. It could be as little as being grateful for having a cup of coffee, or how awesome the weather was today. Or a special hug that I received from my daughter. Or the fact that my husband cooked me a nice meal for dinner, or that I signed up a certain client, or that I made a wonderful presentation to a room of business owners. It can be anything. It doesn't have to be just really big things that you're grateful for in your life, it can be any tiny trivial thing that you say you're grateful for. If you do this daily, you will find that abundance will find its way to you. You're practicing abundance through gratitude. When you're grateful you're abundant in every sense. In your mind and your body and your soul. Nothing really is missing and you never focus on anything that is missing, you just keep going forward and you go "what else can I find?" and what you find is that you start noticing the things that you're grateful for. You start wondering what is it today? What am I going to be writing in my gratitude journal tonight? It only takes 2-3 minutes to write those ten things. It really helps to look back through them, now that I've got 200 days straight. I look back on it and I almost remember those days when those things happened.

So practice gratitude. If you can pick out three of the things that I have shared with you and then work on adding to it over time, you will make changes. Do the little, small 1%-ers. Change one thing at a time and then another until it becomes repetition and it starts embedding your subconscious with those new, positive, money-beliefs.

You need to have that abundance mindset, because in order to make that global difference, you do need some cash flow to be able to get out there and present to the global stage I trust all of this has been helpful and I'd love to hear what you think of this chapter in terms of the actions that you will take and what changes these have created in your life subsequently.

Go forth and love money!

Chapter 13

Bonus Interview with Russell Scott, Author *of Free Time: Business Time Lord Secrets Revealed*

NATASA – As promised, I wanted to bring you the experience of one of the authors who has attended the Ultimate 48 Hour Author Weekend. He has been kind enough to share his time and give us his insights. I have my own perception of how the weekend works but for you, there is benefit in hearing it from someone's experience. So Russell's here to share with us his journey of doing this for the very first time. So Russell, what made you decide to invest in the weekend?

RUSSELL – It was actually a really simple, easy decision, because I know how precious time is. I had a lot that I wanted to share with the broader community and I sort of figured that I don't have time to spend months or even years sitting at a keyboard typing away myself with my two fingers! As soon as I heard about your program to be able to knock it over in a weekend I just jumped at the opportunity.

NATASA – What were you hoping to accomplish by the end of the weekend? Did you have any idea in terms of what was possible and just basically, what was your viewpoint in terms of what you could do?

RUSSELL – Well, I guess I knew it was possible to actually get the whole book knocked over in a weekend, because you've already done it a number of times. The fact that I knew other people had done it made it a lot easier for me to prepare. What I was hoping to accomplish by the end of the weekend was to have all of my content recorded so that I could prepare for the next steps for marketing the book and taking it to the next stage.

NATASA – Awesome! And did you have any writing experience from the past at all?

RUSSELL – Not a lot really. I have to confess that in year 12 English I got a D! And that's not a D for Distinction, that's more a D as barely pass! That's where I come from. I have since then written a few articles and I've written a research paper and so on, so in my career, I have had a need to get involved in some written communication, I've certainly never written any books before.

NATASA – Yeah! It's about doing the practice and putting it out there. I mean I find that the repetition of either writing or whatever you want to perfect as a skill that the experience of getting good at it follows. So well done!

RUSSELL – Thank you and it's also to me a lot about getting really clear on why you want to do it. I've got 40 something years of life experience, so the content is all in me, it's a matter of figuring out (and I have an assistant) to be able to convey that in a compelling manner.

NATASA – So how did you actually find the recording yourself process? Was there something that made it easier? What were some of your strategies? A lot of people might be scared about how they're going to sit down in front of this recorder/phone/computer – worried they might get stuck. What was your opinion and how did you find it yourself?

RUSSELL – I found it to be a really easy and relaxing process. The preparation with the pre-work sheets, I basically had my 12 chapters mapped out, so I had one sheet per chapter. When I sat down with a one-hour block, I had this sheet of paper in front of me that gave me my thoughts, bullet points of what I wanted to cover. I got out my little magic wand microphone, I used a microphone on a laptop. Some other people used a built-in microphone or a phone on a headset. I sort of had the magic wand and just talked in a quiet room without distractions and got my content out there. It was actually really liberating as well because if I was to get up and do a public speech to an audience, then there's all the extra things to worry about, like making sense. If I can put it like that! Getting it all in the right order and using all the right words and everything. This process, by just sitting down and recording, if I've thought of something later on that I wanted to add, I could just record that extra bit. It didn't matter about the sequence, because I could take care of all that in the editing process. It was actually a lot more relaxing than if I was trying to share this in a public speaking type of event.

NATASA – Did you ever get stuck and have to pause and how did you regroup yourself?

RUSSELL – I don't think I did get stuck actually. For me it was a matter of, how do I fit it all in? So like I said, if I've got 40 something years worth of life experience, maybe some of your other writers might have a lot less life experience. For me it was about how I figure out the best bits to convey in that half an hour time box that I had for each chapter so I didn't actually get stuck. I had the ideas on my sheet, because I'd done the thinking in advance and I just got on with it!

NATASA – Awesome! So in saying that, I guess my next question is how important was the pre-work in unpacking your chapters and researching what you wanted to talk about?

RUSSELL – I say it's very important and to be honest I think I told you on the weekend, I didn't actually spend a lot of hours doing it. In the back of my mind, I was always focusing on it, because I knew the date was coming up, so in the back of my mind it was always there. As I thought of an idea or something I could include in my chapter I'd jot it down but I didn't spend ages and ages staring at a screen or a piece of paper jotting ideas down. The amount of preparation I did is relatively small.

NATASA – How many hours would that be? Would you say 4,5,10 hours?

RUSSELL – I reckon it would be definitely less than 10 hours!

NATASA – Less then 10? That's what I've been saying throughout the book – 6-10 hours for the people that want to do this themselves.

RUSSELL – When we did the unpack we went through and figured out what the 12 chapters were going to have as a general subject matter and unpacked one. I'd sort of experienced that process with you for one of them, which I understand you explained a bit more in one of your other chapters. I was able then to unpack others. It gave me a clearer idea so when I thought of an idea for another chapter I could just plonk it in the place that it needed it to be.

NATASA – That's a nice way, that's great! Did you find enough space to get creative in the house without interruptions? How was the experience?

RUSSELL – Yeah, definitely! I was thinking about it before, when I was looking through the questions you sent and it struck me and might sound a bit odd actually, but the biggest challenge was sharing the bathrooms with everybody! That's not such a big challenge after all. I didn't really find a challenge in terms of writing a book. Everybody had space to be able to do things and we were all in the zone.

NATASA – So what was your intention behind writing a book? What do you want to achieve with it? I just want you to share with the readers.

RUSSELL – The first thing that came up for me with this was basically, for me to have an opportunity to share my message and share insights. I've been doing my thing for a bunch of years now and figure I'm reasonably good at it. I wanted to get the message out there and help other people to be able to learn some of the things I've learnt, from the mistakes I've made. I wanted to get my message out there. I want to increase my credibility and stimulate different conversations as well. Each time since I've said to people that I'm writing a book or written a book or whatever, they said that's interesting! Such a small percentage of the population have actually written a book. The minute you've actually done that, it puts you in an exclusive group, an exclusive community.

NATASA – That's correct and that's what I always try to indicate to people who are just thinking about it because there's really nothing to think about because at the end of the day, that percentage is always going to be that low. It takes a lot of courage to actually step up and do it. This brings me to the next question. Have you tried to write a book yourself before? Have you started and stopped or not at all?

RUSSELL – No, not at all. I did add it to my list of goals last year to have a series. My intention is to have a series of books actually. When I was chatting with Blaise, the publisher, she said that quite often people find it addictive. Once they've written a first one they want to go onto the next one and start talking as I am.

NATASA – Yeah, exactly! I'm a living, breathing proof of it! Fourth and the fifth in my mind!

RUSSELL – It is so much fun isn't it?

NATASA – Yes, and as we're recording this interview, I'm nearly done with this book. We've got to do a few more chapters for it, but literally once I've set my mind to it I get it knocked over in about a week and we can get the transcriptionist onto it and get it fine-tuned and off to the publisher, which is wham bam thank you ma'am! It's as easy as that. So what was your aha moment from this experience? Anything that really stood out for you?

RUSSELL – The main thing that stood out is the time box. How on the weekend you set aside the one-hour block and in that one-hour block it's 30 minutes on one chapter 30 minutes on another. It's all laid out there, you put your thing in there, you talk into the microphone for 30 minutes, all right, that chapter's done now! Instead of, I imagine the way that other people might write books, they'll sit there, they'll type away and they'll go back and re-read it and wordsmith it and go to-ing and fro-ing for ages and ages and they might have one chapter done in the amount of time we knock out the whole book.

NATASA – Yes, I know, because the first book I wrote was exactly like that and now in the amount of time it would have taken me to do one chapter, probably two chapters, I'd do a whole book in terms of doing it through this system. That's a really cool one and did you enjoy it? Was it good that it was broken up into teach segments and then obviously writing/recording? Did you like that from a set-up point of view?

RUSSELL – Yeah, definitely. I mean when I sum it all up, I ended up with about just under seven hours worth of recording and so that will turn into my book and how quickly I talk, I don't know how many words will come out. Just under seven hours worth of recording in the Ultimate 48 Hour Weekend. If I'd sat down to talk into the computer for seven hours it would have been exhausting, I think. So having the one hour chunks mixed up with some education, mixed up with some relaxation, chatting, meals, all the other sorts of bits and pieces, it provided the energy. In between the sessions we were chatting with others in the house we could joke around and relax a bit and support each other. We could bounce ideas off each other and celebrate each other's successes like *you've done six chapters and say that's great*. So it was really easy the way it's mapped out. It was really easy to manage our energy levels, I found.

NATASA – That's excellent! So on that note you said that you did form a bond with the other authors that were going through this same experience?

RUSSELL – Yeah, definitely! I mean some of their topics were less relevant to me, some are more so, but we're all on the same journey, so it's a fantastic group to be a part of and it's great to be able to celebrate the successes when they sort of post on Facebook their book cover or whatever. Wow, it looks so cool! And even thinking about who I know that might actually be interested in their book, because I've got that connection with the person that was writing it. Right from that point, the connections we're starting to establish between us, it's not just words on a page, it's a story that's got a heart and soul in it from that person.

NATASA – Yeah, it's like now you're in this exclusive club and you know ten or twelve other authors. You feel like you know the person behind that name, which is a really cool thing. So what advice could you have for other business owners who may be deciding if they should consider the Ultimate 48-hour weekend?

RUSSELL – Well, if you think you've got a message that is worth sharing and you just didn't know how to do it, it is simple, easy and it is so much fun when you do it and you follow the system. It was a blast, wasn't it?

NATASA – Yeah. I can't wait to run the next one! I'm so excited about it.

RUSSELL – Exactly!

NATASA – So about the weekend. Were your needs and requests met in terms of what you wanted in terms of housekeeping, food, what you wanted. Is that okay?

RUSSELL – Yeah, it was more than okay. It was all taken care of. Whether it was wanting to go and grab a cup of tea or coffee, if we wanted to. Meals were taken care of, Stuart did a fantastic job with that. The cooperation, the collaboration, the conversations around the table helped us to stimulate ideas as well. And the space was great. Sharing the rooms, one night, we were just staring at the ceiling with the lights out, chatting and tossing ideas around of what we're going to finish recording the next day.

NATASA – And I think the conversations went on very late into both nights and there were some cool learnings, even in the casual fun times that added value to the weekend. I was very excited about and it was really nice to have that more informal hang-out time where you could build those bonds even stronger. So that's cool!

RUSSELL – Yeah, definitely! Because if you were to do it on your own and follow your system on your own, like spend an hour doing the recording and then an hour maybe watching an educational video or something, you'd miss out on the opportunity to sort of bounce ideas off the other people who are sharing the same journey as you.

NATASA – That's truly the power of the mastermind. When you have twelve people in a room (I'm thinking of the ten authors plus Stuart and me), there's really that mastermind group where if you've got a challenge another person may have the solution that you haven't thought of before.

RUSSELL – Exactly!

NATASA – So that's the added value!

RUSSELL – Exactly, like they say, there's no such thing as a stupid question! There would have been somebody else in the room who asked the question that might have been near the tip of my tongue and it got answered and maybe it got answered by yourself or Stuart or it might have been answered by one of the other authors in the room as well, as we all refer to ourselves as authors now!

NATASA – Of course!

RUSSELL – So those questions were out there and got answered.

NATASA – So do you think people who read this book would be able to follow the steps and reach completion as easily as you would attending that weekend, or even doing it on their own?

RUSSELL – Well I think that if they're committed to the purpose of the book then you can do anything on your own! If they read your book and follow the system, yes, they could achieve the same results, but if they did it by coming to the weekend they'd achieve it even better! If your objective is to get a book out there, there's a few ways you can do that. If your objective is to be able to find some work and have a lot of fun doing it and connecting with some really interesting people along the way, then go to the weekend!

NATASA – Yeah! I truly believe that people can choose either and one has got more of a community and support base. Obviously there's a whole project management side to this that we take care of in terms of the publishing, transcription and website people that we've already sourced and sorted out so people don't need to think about any of those things. I guess those are the pros in that regard! Definitely people can I truly believe, after all I did mine on my own! Once you know the system. My next question was do you think you'll write another book with this system in the future?

RUSSELL – Yeah, definitely.

NATASA – That's what I thought!

RUSSELL – Unless I can find a faster way!

NATASA – Exactly! Well you could cut it right down to the 7 hours, couldn't you, because that's pretty much all the recording you do to get about 40-45,000 words, which is a reasonable-sized book. So what was your biggest challenge over the weekend?

RUSSELL – Some of it was second-guessing myself. Worrying about, what if I leave something important out? What if I say things in the wrong order? What if? What if? What if? And I was saying that it's so liberating because it's about getting the work out there, then when we're in the editing phase I'll get the transcription back. What I actually found was I recorded the 12 chapters and then the introduction and then the conclusion and then I spent a bit more time recording probably another half an hour's worth of extra bits that by the Sunday I'd thought of things I should have included in what I recorded on the Friday or Saturday, so I just recorded them as well. So once I've got the words back from the transcriptionist I can slot those in anywhere I like! If I have something that I've said in chapter 4 that I think belongs in chapter 8, it's just so easy to move! While I was second-guessing myself a little bit, once I realised that stuff it, just put it out there! Fine-tune a little bit later and keep that around a time-box as well. I sort of set myself a window of time that makes sense to do the editing, because I could keep editing and making it better for years if I wanted to, but what's the point of that! I want to get the book out; I've got the time-frame in mind that I want to get the book out! Second-guessing was initially the biggest challenge, but it's just so easy to get over that, I found.

NATASA – You may question yourself in the beginning until you get into the flow of it and then you build that confidence and it's like that old saying where you know you do the do and as you're doing it you become better. So that was similar to myself starting my first chapter over the weekend. The first go I had at it I was a bit rusty because it had been maybe about nine months since I did this for my other book. I was totally unhappy and I was thinking how I was going to get through the whole book! But then I just started it again and had another go. I just visualised myself hosting an amazing workshop for people. I put myself in the zone and my husband was in the other room and he said that was so much better! Then I deleted the first go. Every day I did a chapter or two in a spare hour here or there. It's just coming across, because I can get into that zone. Was there something that you specifically did just before you started recording a chapter?

RUSSELL – Yeah. I did a little bit of juggling actually! If anybody reading this thinks you can't juggle, well neither can I. I drop the balls all the time! But I learned a while back, that juggling is a symmetrical activity with your body. You've got to use the left side and right sides of your body together to be able to juggle, so a couple of minutes of juggling gets the connections in the left side and right side of the brain fired up and I don't know! It might be complete rubbish, but it works for me!

NATASA – That's a really cool tip! You never know, you're focused and as you said, that was a really interesting explanation and I guess everyone would have a different strategy for themselves. I think it's better to do something than not do anything. I know one of the other authors, she had her first sentence constructed, so that she would know how she would start the chapter so then everything would go from there. She found that she needed to get into that flow. Then another person said to me when they felt like they couldn't record 20-30 minutes straight, she would just do a section at a time and once she started doing the sections, she started speaking longer and longer, each time and then she was all of a sudden doing full chapters. Awesome! So you did complete your entire book in the 48 hours didn't you?

RUSSELL – I did! One of the goals I set for myself on Friday, I'd written down and visualised all of the chapters, the files sitting in Dropbox, ready to send to the transcriptionist. That was the goal I set for myself on Friday. I could see that and hear the conversations and felt really good that I got a sense of completion. That's exactly where I ended up with on the Sunday. It was all there. Another thing I noticed as well after the Sunday, as often happens when you've done something, is more ideas came to me! So I just set myself a blank document, so when those ideas came up, I just jotted them down in there! When I get the files back from the transcriptionist probably any day now, I can just add those in as well. Instead of worrying about whether I leave something out or not, I told myself that if it was important, when I think of it, I'll jot it down and add it in!

NATASA – That's so true! So all those people suffering from the perfectionist syndrome. What do you have to say to them in terms of letting go, because I always say to people, do a great job and then fine-tune and clean up your book to the best of your abilities, but there is a point in time that you have to let go. What strategy do you use for yourself to just let it go? Because as you said you could spend the next 5-10 years trying to refine a book before you release it.

RUSSELL – Yeah, exactly! And if you've got a fantastic book in you that never gets written then it's not going to help anybody. The key thing is the time box. For recall, I've got half an hour to put down as much of the great content as I can in that half an hour then I move on! When the transcription comes back and I want to do some word smithing and fine-tuning I do the same thing. So set a time limit around it. Focus on when you want to have the books in the shops. By Christmas? Or to be able to have that box of books just picked up from the mailbox or whatever to be able to start posting out your pre-release versions. What date do you want to have that? So what date do you need to have finished the editing? So always setting that end in mind and working towards that, that will put that time-pressure on yourself to hand it over. And commit to it! So have a set date and commit to it, because the only person that you're cheating is yourself.

NATASA – Exactly!

RUSSELL – People out there need your message and they need it in whatever shape or form it is now. Just know that each and every book you write in the future will be better as you grow and improve and learn and expand your intellectual property.

NATASA – Awesome!

RUSSELL – The other thing that came up for me was the accountability. We finish the weekend on the Sunday. Two days later I sold the first copy of my book. Now the fact that I've sold it and actually received the money motivates me to pull the finger out and finish it, doesn't it? So having the system to be able to set up a pre-sales is great. How we communicate with people about the pre-sale prices, doing our video for the website and getting the website up, all of that put in place, it makes it even more real and I'm not just accountable to myself for finishing the book and finishing it quickly, I'm accountable to the number of people that have already paid the money to buy the book as well!

NATASA – Exactly right and I always say that's the cure for procrastination! Make a commitment to someone else and then you've got to follow through! You have no choice, these people have invested in you, they're committed to you and so you have to be committed to them! There's no procrastination there. Its' very important to earn back your investment on some of the program early! As you're paying it off through your first couple of hundred books that you're going to sell! So I'm always thinking when I invest in something, *how quickly can I get my return on investment?*

RUSSELL – Absolutely agree!

NATASA – How would you describe the weekend in a few words?

RUSSELL – Cool! How would I describe the weekend? Creative, inspiring and supportive!

NATASA – Excellent! And then how would you rate your whole experience out of 10 and if you had any final thoughts I'd love to hear them as we wrap up.

RUSSELL – I could talk for hours on this, but to sum it up, it was fantastic! I'd definitely give it a 10 out of 10! And I also figure it's a metaphor for life as well. If you're going to go out there and do something you do the best you can at the time, get it out there and then next time do it even better. That's what we're doing with this system that you've got for us with the book! If you apply that to anything else you're doing as well, you're going to progressively move forwards.

NATASA – Exactly right! The first weekend that I hosted and then subsequently, say the fifth or the tenth that I host, is going to be a whole different feel and progress and advancement. Same for you. The next book that you write and subsequently the people that you help, as you grow, it's just going to become better and better!

RUSSELL – Absolutely, yeah!

NATASA – Wonderful! Well I thank you so much for your time. I've enjoyed hearing the personal version of how you found everything and I wish you all the success with your book, *Free Time: Business Time Lord, Secrets Revealed.* Trying to get that one right!

RUSSELL – Thanks, Natasa!

NATASA – And you know I can only see an awesome business success as a result of this particular book.

RUSSELL – Thank you very much! I really appreciate the opportunity to help and contribute to your book. Hopefully in this conversation your readers will find inspiration to be able to reach a decision about whether this is the time that has come for them to do this now!

NATASA – Yeah! And whoever's ready, I'm here to help them and give them my 100% to them. Awesome!

Russell working on his book

Afterword

Congratulations! You have reached the part of the book that over 97% of people will never reach! Did you know that only 2-3% of people ever finish reading business books and something like 98% of people never get past the first chapter? Well you have done it! And even better, if you have followed all the steps that I have taken you through this book, to get your book completed within 48 hours, you are one of 3% of people that will ever write a book and really leverage their business through it.

It has been an absolute pleasure to bring all this information to you and if I have missed anything, I expect an email and I would love to give you the answers and help you out on this journey. Feel free to friend me on Facebook and join any of my communities. Subscribe to my YouTube channel; go and connect with me on LinkedIn, because I love building relationships with people. My business has grown through just making friends and really going through a process of selling without having to sell. And people just being part of my community and tribe, and treating everything as a lot of fun and excitement and being really casual about it.

My flavour, in terms of business, is to just do it even if you suck! Keep doing it, because the more you do it, the better you'll get. At the weekend I showed the authors my early YouTube videos and I showed them how different I was back then. I often read some of the stuff I've written 2-3 years ago and each and every book that I bring out is better and better and better and I just love the changes that I see within me and I'm sure you will experience in yourself. If you have done everything that I've said and you have come out with your first book, let me know! I'd love to hear about your success and I'd love to get a copy of your book, because even though I helped many through the Ultimate 48 Hour Author Weekend, I love to also have those stories of people who have read the book and done it for themselves and what changes they've experienced in their life and business.

I'd love to hear those stories! That will make me feel amazing because it means I will be making that scale, even beyond people having that connection with me at a one on one or a weekend. So if you haven't gone through all the bits that I have shared with you, go back! Go back to the start, start at Chapter 1 and do one chapter per week. Take the actions in each chapter every week and you know what? In 12-13 weeks you would have completed everything and what's 90 days really in your life? It's not a long time! In 90 days your life can change. Your business can certainly change.

When I wrote my very first book, the book came out as I was having my second baby. I had to go back and start working my business because the floodgates opened and I was in demand. I did everything between breast-feeding. I'd see clients; I'd go back upstairs and luckily I was based at home. Go networking, come back home, and attend to the baby and everything like that. So it is possible! I had an 18-month old running around, a new baby, a growing business and still continued to do so and juggle all of that and it's important that you focus on your big why.

My big why is to be able to provide that lifestyle to my family and to be able to inspire other women to provide financial independence for themselves and their families, because that's where I came from. Very strong women raised me and they instilled that within me. As I do that, I inspire others. I want you to inspire others too! We all have a story to share and if we can share that through our books, if we can then help people through our systems and programs that we've developed, then opportunities like public speaking come about. Imagine being a keynote speaker that inspires others; those are the people that really start shifting the way humanity is going forward and then bring that awareness that we all need. At some stage or another in our lives we need to spread your message. There are people out there who will pay for what you know and what you can teach them.

So congratulations once again, I'm very proud of you for having reached this part of the book. I can't wait to hear from you about your journey, I am here and waiting. I always like to provide a personal service, by getting back to people myself –that is the one thing that I always want to keep in my business.

So I trust that we'll one day connect and become friends and build up that wonderful friendship and relationship.

Have an awesome time and congratulations!

Appendices

Appendix 1. Post 48 Hour Author Weekend Checklist

	Done ✓
Handing in of Chapter Recordings to Transcriptionist	
Organise Book Cover Design with Blaise with 3D Widget ASAP	
Get all Content for Website Completed and handed in to Matt	
Head Shot, Video, Paypal Account to link up to the Website for Purchases & 3D Widget	
Create an A4 Flyer for Manual pre-orders out and about - Fiverr.com	
Finalise any last sections of Book that are not getting Transcribed	
Upon receiving Transcribed work:	
Cut and Paste - Put all in Order in one big Word Document as it would appear in book	
Read through and make sure you are happy with Paragraphing and flow of book	
Hand Manuscript over to Blaise for editing, proofreading, layout and formatting	
Liase with Nat and Blaise to ensure all is in order before approving final	
Keep Actioning Your Pre-Launch Campaign Checklist	
When Book is Approved to go to Print plan your Launch Party	

Appendix 2. Unpacking Chapters

Chapter heading	XXX
4 WHAT IF:	**1 WHY: (Can cover in a different order when delivering)**
Objections and responses (3): O1 R1 O2 R2 . O3 R3	*Benefits (5):* 1 2 3 4 5 *Fact/statistic (1):* *Quotes (2):* *Contrast (1):*
3 HOW: **3 different ways to teach the WHAT**	**2 WHAT:** **Define each term**
1. 2. 3.	
Additional information/resources:	

Appendix 3. Pre-Launch Campaign Spreadsheet

	Monday	Tuesday	Wednesday	Thursday	Friday	Saturday	Sunday
Date:							
Activity:							
Networking							
Article/Blog							
You Tube							
Facebook							
Linkedin							
Twitter							
Database							

About The Author

Natasa Denman was born and raised in Skopje, Macedonia up to the age of 14 after which she immigrated to Melbourne, Australia with her mum. She didn't speak English and found it challenging in the first two years to fit into the new country and culture. Her zest for learning and achievement fast tracked this process and she had high performance results in her academic endeavours.

Natasa has a Bachelor of Applied Science (Psychology/Psychophysiology), Diploma in Life Coaching, NLP Practitioner Certification, Practitioner of Matrix Therapies, holds a Black Belt in Taekwondo and is a Professional Certified Coach (PCC) through the International Coaching Federation.

Being creative and writing books is something she never planned to do. Her passion for business and marketing was the reason she wrote her first book '*The 7 Ultimate Secrets to Weight Loss*' in June 2011. This book put her first business on the map and enabled her husband to join her full time a year later. She is a contributor of 'You Can ... Live the Life of Your Dreams' and a co-author of 'Ninja Couch Marketing'.

Ultimate 48 Hour Author came about as a result of the success books have brought to Natasa's four businesses. Aside from books she has also written five programs and has three Licensed systems that are being utilised by others internationally in their businesses.

Natasa is a mum of two, Judd who is five and Mika two years old. She loves living her Ultimate Lifestyle whilst helping others do the same through the systems, programs and consulting she provides.

Natasa's Websites:

www.ultimate48hourauthor.com.au

www.ultimatebusinessedge.com.au

www.ultimateweightlossbusiness.com

www.ultimateweightloss.com.au

www.ninjabusinesschicks.com.au

Email: book@ultimate48hourauthor.com.au

Ultimate Book Unpack Session Package

Have you Always wanted to write a book and just never knew where to start?

Do you have a wealth of information in your head and don't know how to organise it?

Are you ready to Build the Business of your Dreams through the Power of being a Published Author?

Like anything in life, there isn't skipping any steps when it comes to this process. Often we find doing a Book Unpack Session gives you an idea of what your book will feel and look like when it's done.

You walk away with:

- **The skeleton for your book**
- **Hypnotic name and outline for best marketing results of your business and book**
- **Knowledge on how a book can leverage your business**
- **Ninja Couch Marketing ebook**
- **Ultimate Secrets to Having More Time ebook**

The package alone can change the way you do business.

Total value is $597.

Your Investment Just $97.

email: book@ultimate48hourauthor.com.au
with subject line: Book Unpack Special
(mention you saw this package in this book).

'There are two times in Life: Now and Too Late' –
Terry Hawkins

Natasa as a Speaker

Natasa Denman is The Ultimate 48-Hour Author. After publishing her fourth book early in 2014, she now mentors and coaches speakers, entrepreneurs and business owners to become published authors and become the authority leaders in their fields. With her Brilliant Ultimate 48-Hour Author Blueprint enabling busy professionals to get their book completed within just 48 hours, her program is highly sought after by those who are looking to influence their market and explode their credibility and standing.

Due Out Feb 2015

As a highly skilled business mentor and coach, Natasa knows that writing your book is only just the beginning and utilises her marketing and publicity knowledge to make sure that all of her authors get the results they are looking for with a strategic business plan which outlines the step-by-step process that needs to be followed. With 100% success rate from all attendees at her retreats, The Ultimate 48-Hour Blueprint is the first choice for business owners looking for the competitive edge.

Natasa is a sought after speaker on the following topics:

Author Your Way to Business Success

- How to position a book lucratively for your Brand
- Building Leverage with your book
- The secret to writing your book in just 48 hours

Mumpreneur Secrets to a Profitable Business from Home

- Juggling Babies and business with success
- Replacing selling your time for money for profit
- Finding Flow and Time for Your Ultimate Lifestyle

Ultimate Expert Positioning Formula

- The 3 Keys to positioning as an expert
- One reason why people fail to establish themselves as the expert
- Leveraging your Expert Status for profit

Contact Info: 0412 085 160
www.natasadenman.com
natasa@natasadenman.com

Ultimate 48 Hour Author Retreats	Silver	Gold	Platinum
Mentoring & Accountability			
2 Hour Pre Weekend Prep Session One on One	✔	✔	✔
Unlimited Email Support	✔	✔	✔
Laser Mentoring until Book Release	✔	✔	✔
Ultimate 48 Hour Author Weekend Training & Support Including:	✔	✔	✔
1. Speaking Success System	✔	✔	✔
2. The Power of Social Media	✔	✔	✔
3. Connecting Through Video	✔	✔	✔
4. Free Publicity Generation	✔	✔	✔
5. Successful Publicity Follow Up System	✔	✔	✔
6. Pre-Launch Campaign	✔	✔	✔
7. Your Mindset Success	✔	✔	✔
Essentials for Success	✔	✔	✔
Luxury Accomodation	✔	✔	✔
Restaurant Style Meals	✔	✔	✔
Transcription of Your Book - 7 Hours Max		✔	✔
Webinar Set Up and Promotion to Explode Your Book Sales		✔	✔
Essential Checklist to Prepare You for the Weekend		✔	✔
Checklists/Guides up to Publishing Handover		✔	✔
Pre-Launch Campaign Set Up		✔	✔
Publishing		✔	✔
ISBN/Barcode		✔	✔
Copyeditting (40 000 words max)		✔	✔
Internal Layout		✔	✔
Cover Creation (Including 3D Version)		✔	✔
100 Books (Black and White internal printing)		✔	✔
Author Photoshoot		✔	✔
E-Book Version of the Book		✔	✔
Library Deposit		✔	✔
Bonuses		✔	✔
Ultimate Product Generator Manual and Training Footage		✔	✔
Ninja Couch Marketing & Ultimate 48 Hour Author Books		✔	✔
Social Media Made Easy		✔	✔
Secrets to Running Webinars for Profit		✔	✔
12 Ninja Stars to Business Explosion E-Course (10 Hrs)		✔	✔
10 Easy Steps to Bust Your Money Limiting Beliefs		✔	✔
Ultimate Busines Support Inner Circle Membership Lifetime		✔	✔
One on One Mentoring Support (3 Months)			✔

By Application Only email: book@ultimate48hourauthor.com.au

Free Time: Business Time Lord Secrets Revealed by Russell Scott

Did you start out in business with the aim of getting more free time, and now you find yourself as a slave to the business, working long hours bogged down in the daily details, with little energy left when you are away from the business? If only you had more time! Free time! Free time for you to use however you choose.

http://freetimebook.com.au/

Why Men Made Me Fat: How I Took Back My Power by Alana Carpenter

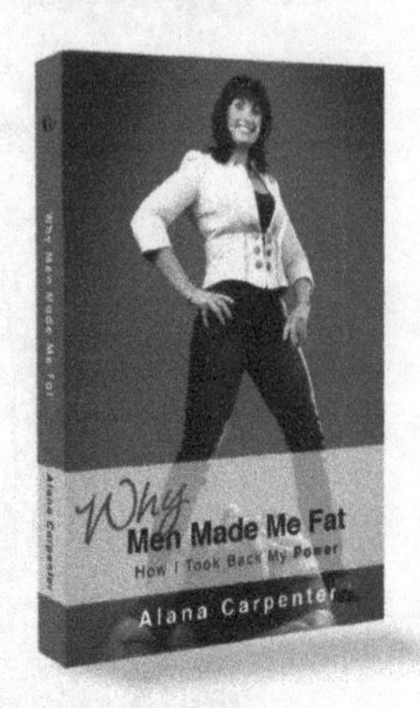

Have you tried everything to lose weight and always wanted to look slimmer and be healthy but didn't know where to start because of life challenges that got in the way?

Or perhaps you see it as this gigantic scary life change so it's always being put in the 'too hard' basket? It doesn't have to be that way.

Losing weight, feeling fit and healthy can be fun, easy and super rewarding.

http://whymenmademefat.com

Quest to Freedom by John Sharkey

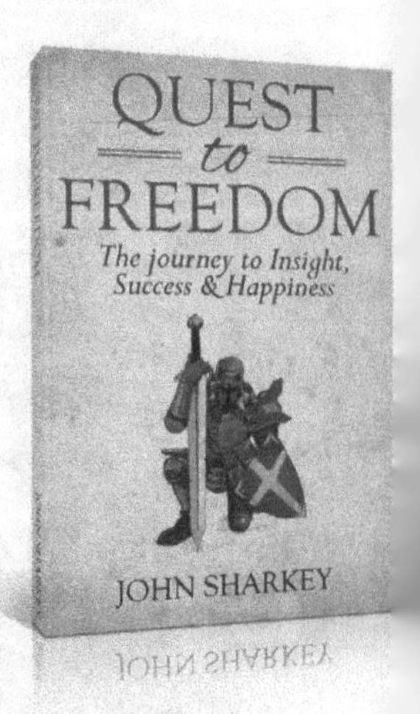

Creating the life, career and relationships you want can seem like a daunting task. With busy modern day living we seem to communicate more and talk less, live in bigger houses and feel less secure, work longer and have less time for what's truly important to us.

You will learn strategies, use exercises and tips that will teach you how to write goals, understand the way you think, find out what's important to you and unlock those blocks in your way. Its time to take backcontrol, and rule over your kingdom like the crusaders of a time gone past.

After all, your life is waiting for you out there to conquer on your 'Quest to Freedom'.

http://johnsharkey.com.au